We Never Lost Hope

A Holocaust Memoir and Love Story

Naomi Litvin

Foreword by Sir Martin Gilbert

For Pun and Cunku

ISBN: 1-4392-0421-7
ISBN-13: 9781439204214
Library of Congress Control Number: 2008906734

Visit www.booksurge.com to order additional copies.

Table of Contents

V   Voice: Naomi

Preface

The five voices in this book belong to **Edith**, **Hilda**, and **Mendi Festinger**, the three youngest born in a large Transylvanian Jewish family; **Nate Litvin**, the American Jewish GI from Michigan who loved Edith; and **Kurt Meyers**, the Dutch Jew from Indonesia that loved Piri, another Festinger sister

Foreword

Naomi Litvin leaves all students of the Holocaust in her debt. The literature on this subject is vast, but so is the subject. Two stories here intertwine. Edith's story is a powerful one. She was born in the same town as Elie Wiesel – Sighet - the youngest of nine children. Her brother Mendi's story is equally powerful. Their respective memories of childhood evoke a rich Jewish past.

In 1939, Edith became a nanny in Budapest for a Jewish family. But with the coming of war she returned home. Soon, Satu-Mare, hitherto a Romanian town, was occupied by the Hungarians. Mendi managed to help the family by starting an Angora rabbit farm: fourteen girls worked for Edith, knitting the wool. In 1942, Polish Jewish refugees reached Satu-Mare. "They were telling us stories," Mendi recalled, "and we wouldn't believe it."

Then came the day when the Jews had to sew yellow stars on their clothes. And then the day when they had to leave their homes and move into a crowded, insanitary ghetto: the whole of Edith and Mendi's family in one room. Next came deportation to Auschwitz. From this moment, the memoirs of Edith and Mendi are poignant in the extreme. The light at the end of the tunnel – a very long and dark tunnel indeed – is their story after liberation, and Edith's love for an American GI: "The two of us were completely one."

No Holocaust memoir is easy to read, and these recollections of Auschwitz and its aftermath make for hard reading. But every memoir adds to our knowledge, both of what happened, and of the emotions and feelings of that terrible era, and this memoir is no exception: it calls out to be read.

Martin Gilbert
24 August 2008

Hopes Worthwhile

I was young my hopes were real
While imprisoned always ill
When bars and wires surrounded me
A pen and paper I needed most
Essays, poems, stories to be told
How could I keep silent one year long

When life was young my hopes were high
And all the world and hopes worthwhile
Gallant men have I not seen
Kisses, love, desires unreal
Even in that place obscene
I was young, my hopes were real

Twenty lashes for that girl
Cried the Nazi commander
Much I cared, it didn't hurt
A look at him, a face absurd

I am hungry, please dear sir
One more lash for that trash girl
I am thirsty, please have mercy
Put that slave on heavy drill
She'll have no bread and much too dirty

Throw her back where she belongs
With all the Jews in piles of mud
It's all right I said to the guard
I have no one so what's the fright

My hopes and dreams kept me alive
My hair will grow, we all will strive
One day we'll have the food we need
Clothes, water, and all I dreamed

Ten men strong against one girl
Ten commandments meant nothing to her
Thou Shall Not Kill, Thou Shall Not Hurt
Honor Thy Parents, repeatedly heard

I'd honor my Father my Mother too
Except they slaughtered them two by two
To hell with you, you dirty Jew
Bellowed the Nazi high from his view

Silent moaning throughout the day
Screams and pain through the night
God is lost on a path to our way
Not up nor down
Nowhere in sight

I was young, my hopes were real
It kept me alive with dreams unreal
I'd think, I'd dream of life's loveliness
And hope someday to receive tenderness

I taught myself to laugh again
Restored my faith in all of men
Spring to me feels more like May
Heaven broke the chains today

On April 13, 1945 Patton's Fourth Armored Division liberated me.
Edith Festinger

Part 1

Chapter One

Sighet is a small and unique old market town, in the county of Maramures, in the region of Transylvania. Sighet, which was founded during the 14th century, is in the northernmost part of Romania in a remote and rural area. Sighet is thirty-seven miles north of Baia Mare, one mile from the Ukrainian border, and where three rivers: the Tisza, Ronisoara, and Iza intersect. Many of the villages around Sighet are unique and reflect old Europe.

∽

EDITH: I was born October 6, 1923 in Sighet, Transylvania. My parents were Regina Stein and Jonas Festinger, who had nine children at the time of World War II. I was the youngest, and they named me Edita, or Edith in the Americanized version. When 'ke', a Hungarian endearment, is added to the name, it becomes Editke and translates to Edith darling. I had a beautiful childhood. All I know about my mother is that she came from Czechoslovakia and her family had settled in Hosszumeszu, Hungary, which translates to Long Prairie. That is where my father lived and my parents met and fell in love there. My parents were very young when they met. My father was very religious and in those days, they married early, because they didn't fool around. My mother must have been around sixteen, seventeen at the most. She was absolutely indescribably beautiful. She had golden blonde hair and very soft features. I don't know what my father looked like as a young man, but he had black hair and they tell me he was very good looking. He was in the wine business and supplied the army with wine.

Mother had ten children before I was born. Two of the babies had died and she suffered three miscarriages. Born between 1904 and 1908, were Zsenka, Aranka, Ceca, Helen, and Hershmila, a boy who drowned in the Tisza River.[1] After a while, maybe around 1911, my parents and their five children moved from the Hosszumeszu area that was close to the border of Czechoslovakia, to Sighet in Romania.

After 1915, came Johnny, Piri, Mendi, and Hilda, and by the time I was born there were nine of us children and my parents living in Sighet. Mother always told me, "A woman is just a mattress." We stayed in Sighet until 1934, and then when I was eleven years old we moved to Satu-Mare. During some of this time in Sighet, we lived at the hotel that Father and Mother owned. Father was very rich, and when he came to Sighet he could have bought any hotel that he wanted, and he wanted the Tisza Hotel, so he bought it.[2]

MENDI: I was born February 22, 1920 in Sighet, Romania. At that time Sighet had a population of 30,000, and 20,000 were Jews. My family were Orthodox Jews who originated in Campulong La Tisa, and went back three hundred years from there.[3] It was Hungary before World War I, then Romania. My parents were Jonas and Regina Festinger. During World War I, Jonas was a wine dealer who supplied the Hungarian Army and then after the first war he bought a hotel in Sighet. The address of our hotel was 60 Ferdinand Street in Sighet.

EDITH: Mother was a very superstitious person. During her entire pregnancy with me, she was having a recurrent dream in which the town whore, who had recently died, came to her crying and complaining about her unhappiness. It was Etya Sasa and she was wandering around between worlds with no peace. She had been a local Jewish girl who had just gone the wrong way in life, and now was apparently living in Regina's dreams. There was a story handed down that said that if a spirit haunted you while you are pregnant, then you should name your child after that ghost and that will solve the haunting and the ghost will find peace. And so that is how I got my Hebrew name.

My earliest memories are of Sighet. I remember my oldest brother Johnny bathing me in a little bucket, out in the sun, in the open in the backyard. It was summertime; the water was warm. I must have been very small; I couldn't have been more than a few years old. He must have loved me very much. He was washing my hair and he picked me up and put a towel around me. All of my brothers and sisters should have been watching out for me and parenting me because I was the youngest, the baby. But really, I think that they just let me run wild. By that time they must have been tired of little children.

Also, as soon as I could start walking, we walked over to Czechoslovakia, especially during Passover. Sighet was walking distance to the border, across the river. If you went swimming, you said hello to the Czechs. And above the bridge there were the soldiers, the police guards. We went over that bridge to see the Bata Shoes, that famous shoe company. I was walking with my mother, always with Mother. We would go to Father's sister's house and knock on the door, and there would be my Aunt Rivka and the cousins. They were all better people, you know? I don't remember the name of the town, but Czechoslovakia was very beautiful and very promoted.

At the hotel we had a Gypsy doorman whose name was Oden. He was a concierge that had been with us for years and years. He was very close to us. He went out across to the railroad station when the trains came in with his helpers, calling out, "Tisza Hotel, Tisza Hotel," advertising our hotel. And they would grab the traveler's suitcases and let the people follow. And right next door to the Tisza Hotel was the Katz Hotel, another Jewish hotel, and they were also at the train station yelling for their hotel, so my father and them never spoke. They were always feuding. But the son of the owner of the Katz Hotel was my best friend; the children were always at peace.

Some of the other most memorable times of my early childhood were with my little boyfriend from next door. We were climbing apple and all kinds of other trees. We were always running around and having marvelous times. I remember going next door. His mother was cooking strawberry jam and it smelled and tasted like heaven. She looked at me and she gave me a piece of bread with strawberry jam on top. We had strawberries and raspberries growing in the backyards. And the little boy and I would walk together holding hands and swinging our hands as we went across the street from the two hotels to the railroad station. They had those bars, like handrails, there that you could climb onto. All the kids played on those bars, and there was a water fountain there, but I wasn't tall enough to reach the fountain to get a drink. I was so jealous of the bigger kids that could reach for a drink of water! Once in a while a grown-up would lift me up so I could get a drink. So I just climbed onto the bars and hung on with my legs and swung back and forth by my knees like the monkeys do. I must have been three or four years old, and I had little panties on and while I was swinging my dress went over my head. Like did I care? I was very jealous that the little boy could wear pants! Sometimes I would see Oden and he would start yelling, "Editke, Editke, your mother wants you!" And I would yell back at him, "Go away, I am playing now!" And one time he grabbed me off the bars and carried me home to The Tisza Hotel.

The rooms at the hotel were on one level with a multitude of windows. It was very bright. The main rooms were set aside for the Festinger family. The largest room was designated as a living room for the Festingers and they referred to it as Number Two. To our family, Number Two was the most beautiful room in the entire hotel and that is where the family gathered. Each room had a colorful hand-woven rug in it. There were many bedrooms: some for the children, some for the parents and other relatives and travelers. All the rooms were typical hotel rooms and were kept very neat. The outside of the hotel was built out of brick. Since all the rooms had fireplaces, a lot of wood was needed which was chopped and stacked by employees after being bought from men that came by with the wood on wagons. The dining room and the kosher kitchen were very large and busy.

All of my brothers and sisters were involved in the hotel operations. There was much to do with guests to receive and feed, and baggage to take care of. My sister Aranka was an advisor with the restaurant: as to what types of food to buy and supervising the cook in the kitchen. My brother Johnny was in charge of the payroll and the bookkeeping. With plenty of room, the Festinger relatives from other villages in Hungary and Czechoslovakia always found shelter in our hotel, whether attending school or while looking for work. Travelers were plentiful at the Tisza Hotel until economic conditions began to deteriorate.

I remember my first day of school; I asked to go to the bathroom and they wouldn't let me. I pished on the floor. I was very embarrassed and I cried. And the teacher patted my head and said, "It's o.k. Honey, it's o.k." I looked up in her face and saw that she was very nice, and very tall.

The boys went to Cheder, Jewish school, and the Rabbi beat the boys with a stick. The girls were lucky. We didn't have to go. Usually a male member of the family would teach the girls the Hebrew prayers. My father paid me off to learn those prayers. Ten lei! It was a lot of money in those days. And then I would run to the outdoor kiosk that was a candy stand with the money. My favorite candy was the halvah, made out of crushed sesame seeds, honey, cream, butter, and tahini. If Mitzi Nanee, the woman who ran the candy stand, got drunk early, then we didn't need any money and we filled our pockets with hazel nuts and all kinds of suckers.

MENDI: During my childhood I started to go to Cheder when I was four years old. At six I started primary school, then at ten I went to high school.

In Sighet there was a small synagogue every few streets. The Rabbi close to our house was a brother of the famous Satmar Rabbi. But during that time, my father was a disciple of another Rabbi from Poland,

The Antonera Rebbe, and from time to time he came to Sighet and would stay at my parents' hotel with us.

EDITH: When I was little, Father would take out his handkerchief and make a rabbit head out of it to entertain me. One time I had the measles and that was when the circus came to town. Father was making wet compresses for my head because I had a high fever and he laid me down on my bed. And then I looked out of the window and there was a giant man from the circus, the one that wore high shoes, like stilts, and he poked his head into the window and said to Father, "What is the matter with the little girl?" I said, "I have the measles," so he took out a chocolate bar from his pocket and gave it to me. I was out of my mind with happiness! And the next thing I saw were all the animals marching down the street. They had the elephants loose and the lions were in cages in a truck and there were all kinds of monkeys! It was tremendous excitement for me. It was a very famous circus, some of the circus people had come from Romania, and they traveled all around Europe to the other countries.

MENDI: Father was a very gentle man who wouldn't hurt a fly. One time he captured a small mouse in our house, and I remember that he carried that little mouse outside and set it free.

Most of the Festinger children went to Indonesia prior to World War II. In 1930, my brother-in-law Willie Lillian, and my eldest sister Zsenka went to Indonesia for one year. Their two children, Johnny and Elsa stayed with us, and then their parents came and took them back to Indonesia.

EDITH: By this time my sisters Zsenka, Ceca, and Helen were married and living in Java. Zsenka was the first Festinger to go to Java. She had gone with my brother-in-law, Willie Lillian. He and his friend, Jules de Leeuw had traveled to Java together. They were telling stories about diamonds and jewelry and all that stuff. Willie was from all over; I don't know which country exactly, just the same as us. Willie met Zsenka at Hosszumeszu in Hungary when he was a Captain in the Hungarian Army and he bought wine from Father. He fell in love with her and they were married and had a baby before I was born. My sister scared me to death, because she was the oldest and I was the youngest. And I didn't dare call her by her name because of our age difference.

Helenke had a boyfriend before she went to Java. He was Cirimis, the big King of the Gypsies. Zsenka found out from Father that this was going on, it was very scandalous, and then she sent for Helenke and according to family legend, that is how Helen went to Java. And then I suppose she met Jules de Leeuw through Willie Lillian.

MENDI: In 1934 my sister Helen had married a very rich jeweler. His name was Jules de Leeuw. The family in Indonesia wrote regularly to our parents and it was during the depression when Jules found out how bad conditions were for us in Sighet. He sent an amount of money to pay off the debts of my parents. The debts were taxes owed and then from then on he sent a certain amount every month, which solved our problems. There was a lot of poverty in Sighet and when we were doing well we had a soup kitchen. A lot of poor people came and ate. Father also gave them a bit of money.

EDITH: In the Tisza Hotel, the front parts of the hotel were all businesses that were rented out. There was a butcher, but it was not a kosher butcher, a baker, and a shoemaker; and one space that became a candy store. When my brother-in-law Jules de Leeuw came from Indonesia, since he was always the boss man and he needed something to do, he took over that store and made it a candy store. In it he carried cigarettes and breadstuff, and all the things that travelers would want to buy: bon-bons, chocolate bars, all kinds of candies. That was very exciting; we all got such a kick out of it!

Another most memorable time is when my sister Helenke was ready to give birth to a baby. She told her husband Jules de Leeuw that she insists on delivering the baby in her mother's house, at the Tisza Hotel. So they traveled all the way from Bandung in Indonesia to Sighet. They brought a beautiful American car with them. It was a white convertible with red leather interior. Father had a garage built especially for that car. He hired carpenters and they came to the hotel to build the outdoor garage. Jules had picked up his mother in Dartmouth and brought her to Sighet for the baby's birth. She stayed with us in the hotel. I remember she was soaking her feet in a tub, and I helped to massage her feet. She was a very nice lady.

We had a midwife to help with the birth of Evelyn, Helenke's baby. They said to me, "Do you smell that thing? Goya Goya, huszu lobu goya, that's a big bird, a stork with the long legs! The stork is coming, he is above the house and he is just delivering the baby to your sister." I suppose the smell was the medicine that came from the room.

This time, in Sighet, I was still a little girl about five years old. We were crammed into Jules' car. It was packed with people. There were three in the front and five, six, or seven of us kids in the back, and a few people just hanging on to the sideboards! Jules had a little tiny folding chair that he put on the back seat floor for me. My sister Hilda didn't come with us; she was a bad girl that day and Jules made her stay at home. We drove to Hungary, to Father's hometown, the village of Hosszumeszu. As we arrived in the center of town Jules ran down and killed all the chickens that were in the street! He was laughing and taking great joy in this awful killing of chickens and the Romanian peasants were yelling at him. They said, "God will get you for this. Someone will do this to you!" Then he went into a Christian butcher shop and purchased all kinds of non-kosher salami and cold cuts, like kielbasa. It was the first time that I ate meat that wasn't kosher.

Eugene Schwartz, who was a cantor, fell in love with my sister Aranka, but she did not fall in love with him. They met through Ceca's husband, Miki Meyer, who was Eugene's first cousin. They all talked Aranka into marrying Eugene. She was like that.

On her wedding day, I played a nasty trick on Aranka. I was seven years old, and I said, "Aranka, why don't you sit down on this chair?" And when she went to sit down, I pulled the chair out and she fell on the floor in her wedding gown. They always lived with us, with their son Freddie, except when they went to Java and had very bad luck and did not do well there. They returned to Romania and lived in the Tisza Hotel. Then also, later on we were separated when they went traveling to Bucharest, Romania and we were accidentally separated by politics.

The food at our hotel was the best! We had people, such as Oden and my brothers that went to the Sighet market place in the center of town to buy large quantities of ingredients for the hotel kitchen and restaurant. We had all the delicious Hungarian kosher foods like stuffed cabbage, borscht, paprikash, and Hungarian goulash. The pastries were all exquisite varieties. Coffee was served with desserts in little demitasse cups.

We had hired a special cook for the people that visited us. Her name was Mareshka and she was very tall and very fat. In fact her touchas was so big that I used to love to follow her around and hide behind it so no one could see me. I held on to her skirts and apron and she would try to kick me and try to shake me away, saying "Skat!" And I would say to her, "Shush, Mareshka!" and then I even kicked her to shut her up. She always had her hands full, with trays of stuffed cabbage or other delicacies. The dining room was so elegantly set, always. I remember eating there and my brother-in-law Jules telling everyone, "How beautiful that child eats." We served three meals daily for the hotel guests. And the maids washed the dishes. A lot of maids were running around, cleaning rooms and there were maids that stayed in the kitchen all the time. There was always a lot of commotion! There were a lot of employees, for the hotel and for our family's use. There was one maid to take care of me, because I was the youngest. And she would take me walking, and teach me dirty words in Russian, "Hu ze cu" which meant kiss my ass. And so I went telling people, "Kiss my ass" in Russian, and so a stranger would yell at me, "You dirty little girl!"

Emma was a maid that was cleaning rooms and she was also a prostitute. Her customers were men that came to the hotel. It was talked about; there was gossip about Emma! I could hear my brothers and sisters talking about her, and I was listening. I remember seeing her a lot, bumping into her, always fooling around with her. She was funny and very nice. She used to keep a chocolate bar in her bosom and when she saw me, she put her hand inside her bosom and pulled out the chocolate bar and gave it to me. The chocolate would be soft from the heat of her bosom, but I didn't care. She was laughing a lot and finally she disappeared because one of the men that she saw a lot married her.

My grandfather lived with us and he was really bad. He was chasing women. He had lost his wife before then. Grandmother had died suddenly from being burned in a fire. He was very religious and he was chasing the whores. There were stories going around about him. He had a reputation and everyone knew about his sexual appetite. He always carried rock candy in his pocket.

MENDI: Joseph Festinger was our paternal grandfather. He moved in with us in Sighet after Grandmother died suddenly, accidentally in a fire. Grandfather lived with us for the rest of his life.

Father wrote Purim plays in verse, and actors in the Jewish Theatre performed some of them on stage. I was about twelve or thirteen when he wrote the last one.

From time to time we always had visitors and some relatives were practically brought up with us in our home. Conditions during these times in the 1930's were very bad because of the Depression.

People didn't travel and many times the hotel was empty. I didn't have a winter coat.

EDITH: The kitchen of the Tisza Hotel had a Dutch door and faced out to the large back courtyard. There were ten small bungalows out in the back yard that Father rented out to various local people. Some of the tenants worked for the railroad. We rented out the little houses in the back yard to families and to single people too. That is where Mitzee Nanee lived. And there was a bathroom out there that had about five toilets in it. One of the little houses had some Christians living there and they had some little piglets and a mother pig. One time right before a Christmas two guys ran after one of the pigs so they could slaughter it, and chop up the meat and prepare it for wintertime. Finally after a lot of running around and the pig squealing a lot they finally caught him. They stuck a knife in the pig and the blood started running out of it. They had all these buckets that they put under the pig to catch the blood because Hungarian peasants cooked in the blood. And they hung up all the cuts of the pig outside because they didn't have any refrigeration, and they had to dry and smoke the meats, like ham and all that. I used to sit in their kitchen and watch the mother cook up certain things like bellies and sew up certain parts to make kielbasa and foods like that. It smelled like heaven but I didn't taste anything.

We had a cow and her name was Laba and she gave birth to a calf and the calf was dancing around in the water hole in the courtyard, behind the hotel, near where the well was, where we kept the watermelon cold. I was so sad and crying at one time because

Father sold the calf, whose name was Buba. So I called the chickens and the geese over to me and as it was my job to collect the greens to feed them, they came to me very easily. So on this day that Buba was sold, I quickly forgot about the calf. I took my special basket and went collecting the eggs. The duck eggs were bigger than the chicken eggs and the geese eggs were bigger yet. That reminds me of the maid feeding the goose to fatten up the liver. She was outdoors and she was sitting on the ground. She put her leg on top of the goose's neck and held the head with her hand and she fed the corn into its mouth and then took her finger and put it in the goose's mouth and pushed the corn down. And when it finally reached the goose's neck, she massaged by the outside and finally gave the goose a chance to relax and rest up. We bought the geese in order to stock up food for the winter.

The back area had room for fruit and vegetable gardens, cows, and other livestock. I don't remember any flowers growing around the hotel, but when you went into the backyard it felt magical, like you were in a different area. This was where all the stuff was growing; vegetables, fruit, berries. It was a big place.

Because Father was still in the wine business he kept wine barrels in the cellar. When there were floods, we went down to the basement through the back entrance and sat on the barrels and rode around in the water.

The most vivid thing that I remember is that we used to go out in the backyard and we could see the windows into each hotel bedroom. When we knew that a guest came, or a couple, a man and a woman, we climbed up on the top of the cellar and you could see right into the bedroom. One time I saw a man climbing on a woman. I was a little child and I had my girlfriend with me and we both watched. The man had those peasant, heavy jackets and coats that were made out of woven lamb fur and embroidered with beautiful Romanian designs. And he didn't even take them off; he just climbed onto the woman with all those clothes on. And then I saw them walking out and paying for the room. I knew what they were doing because my little boyfriend from next door always talked about that stuff, especially since we always saw the dogs doing it.

One day I saw Father lying in the backyard naked. I think he had high blood pressure or something like that and he was told that sunshine would be good for him. So he was undressed naked, just laying there, getting some sun by the raspberry bushes. So I was telling my girlfriend, "Look at my father, he is eating raspberries, laying there naked."

Downtown Sighet had a movie house. We children went to the movies with our class from school or chaperoned by older relatives, as we were not allowed to go by ourselves. On the school days that we were to go to the movie, the principal would send out a little red book for us to sign. One girl would come to the door of the classroom and give it to our teacher. When we saw that red covered book we were all jumping from joy! And the teacher would read to us about the movie that we were going to see at three o'clock in the afternoon. And then the teacher would lead the way, and we girls would go down the street in pairs. The first movie I saw in Sighet had a lot of Mickey Mouse cartoons with it. It was The Singing Fool with Al Jolson.[4] He sang, "Sonny Boy, Sonny Boy... La La La La'... It was an American movie and they were speaking English and there were Hungarian subtitles.

One time the whole family was going to the movies and everyone had a ticket except for my sister Piri. So I gave my ticket to her and I stayed home. I could never forget that. I had a good heart by then. And it was easy with Piri. She was so very lovable; she was everyone's favorite. You could always find her laughing and dancing.

At school in those days, we girls had embroidery as part of the curriculum. One time I had the assignment of embroidering a beautiful, ornate design on a pink blouse. There was a Jewish farm girl who lived in one of the very nearby villages and she was in love with my brother Johnny, but Johnny didn't love her back. Jewish farmers were unusual, Jews were seldom farmers. This farm girl, because she was trying to get Johnny's attention, helped me to iron that pink blouse and when I went to her house, I saw that next door to her farm lived a family of Romanian peasants. That family had had a tragedy; their two boys had been struck by lightening and killed. The Romanian funeral was lasting three days with tremendous amounts of food and heavy drinking, and a lot of crying. So, I went over there with her.

MENDI: At school we spoke Romanian with our teachers. At home we spoke Yiddish with our parents. With my two younger sisters, Hilda and Edith, and with our friends we spoke Hungarian. We also learned Hebrew and at school we had a choice of taking either Italian or English, and I chose English. We also learned French and German. I could also write in all of the languages.

EDITH: Every year on December 16, it was Saint Nicholas' day. We called him Nicholas Baci. All the children put their shoes outside, on the windowsill, even the Jewish children. And if we didn't behave ourselves we knew that we would find stones in our shoes. I never got stones; I always got all the delicious chocolates and candies in my shoes. My brother Johnny took care of carrying on that tradition.

Chapter Two

In 1931, the Festinger family moved from the Tisza Hotel to a large home in Sighet. Close to the end of Edith's first year in high school, in 1935, the Festinger family moved again, this time to Satu-Mare, in Northwestern Romania, sixty-two miles north from Sighet on the Somes River. Edith's sister Ceca, brother-in-law Micki Meyer, and their child Greta had settled there after their return from Indonesia, coming back to Romania to establish a gem stone business. The extended family found a house together on Attila Street.

In the 1930's Kurt Meyers, a Dutch Jew, was a jewelry salesman traveling around in the East Indies. Through a friend's recommendation, Kurt had received a letter with a job offer in Jules de Leeuw's company with a nice salary plus commission. Kurt accepted this offer and went from Genoa, Italy on a Dutch ship to the Dutch East Indies. He had arrived in Jakarta in January of 1931 to work for Jules de Leeuw's thriving jewelry business, which was based in Bandung, West Java, 112 miles southeast of Jakarta. Most of their business was done by traveling to smaller islands and places all over Indonesia. Kurt had accompanied Jules and his brother for two months to learn the business and the Malayan language. After training, Kurt was given a car with a chauffeur and he was on his own traveling to Java, Sumatra, the Borneo, Celebes, and all of the other islands. Kurt's clients were rajahs, sultans, and government service people. In 1936, Kurt Meyers went to Europe for vacation and went to Satu-Mare, Romania to meet Piri Festinger, who was Jules' sister-in-law.

On May 10, 1940 the Netherlands were caught up in the Second World War when German troops invaded their country. The Dutch army had surrendered four days later. In the Dutch East Indies the Dutch government had fled to London. By then it had become clear that a Japanese attack on Indonesia was imminent.

Hungary and Romania had joined Hitler's Axis in November of 1940. The 1940 annexation of Northern Transylvania, Romania by Hungary victimized the Transylvanian Jews. They were resented by the Romanians because of their inclination to everything Hungarian, including language and culture. At first, because of recent Romanian anti-Semitism, the Northern Transylvanian Jews had illusions of the return of a Hungarian Golden Era. But the Hungarians soon implemented anti-Jewish laws that had already been in effect in Hungary.

Meanwhile, the bombing of Pearl Harbor on December 7, 1941 inevitably would plunge the Festinger family in Indonesia into the hands of the Japanese as prisoners-of-war. After the defeat of the KNIL's Dutch Army on March 9, 1942, the prisoners-of-war. After the defeat were put into camps near the place where the army had surrendered.[5] In May of 1942 on Sumatra, and starting in October of 1942 on Java, the prisoners-of-war were taken to more remote locations, sometimes as far away as Japan or Manchuria. The treatment to which the Japanese subjected their prisoners caused the deaths of about 8,200 Dutch prisoners-of-war in the hard labor internment camps.

In March and April of 1942, in the Dutch East Indies, the European schools were closed down, and all Dutch newspapers and magazines had disappeared. Soon after the start of the Japanese Occupation, the Japanese interned the entire European civilian population (approximately 80,000 people) on the islands in the archipelago apart from Java - Sumatra, Celebes, Borneo, the Moluccas, and Timor. The women with children were taken to different camps from the men. The internment period lasted three years or more. The internees lived in almost complete isolation from the outside world, in conditions that grew worse every day. 16,800 internees did not come out alive.

By 1942, Jews from all over Europe were in Poland's Ghettos and Death Camps, having been rounded up by Hitler's regime. Most of the ghettos in Poland were already established by the beginning of 1942. Six major concentration/death camps began operations in Poland set up to kill Jews: Lublin, Kulmhof (Chelmno), Treblinka, Sobibor, Belzec, and Auschwitz.

On March 19, 1944 the German occupation of Hungary violently ended the relative safety of the Jews of Northern Transylvania. Hitler was determined to stop Hungary from getting out of the Axis Alliance and to prevent that, he had ordered troops into Hungary. Jonas Festinger had been an ardent follower of Rebbe Yoylash (Joel Teitelbaum), the famous Satmar Rabbi who was anti-Zionist.[6] The Rabbi's followers still hoped that there would be some safety from the German deportations because of prior pro-Jewish Hungarians. But in 1944 they did not realize it was a new generation for Hungarians.

∽

EDITH: Around 1931, when I was about eight years old, we ended up moving from our hotel. During this time my brother Johnny was in the Romanian Army, in the cavalry, and he had a horse. Father was devastated because he wanted to save Johnny from going to war, or wherever they were sending the Jewish boys in those days, and he was willing to do anything in order to save him. Father had a plan to send Johnny to Java to be with the other family members. The war had not broken out yet, but Father knew that it was coming. I suppose he had to bribe some official. That's the way it worked. This tragically affected Mother because this hotel meant everything to her. You know, when you buy something in a marriage, two people sign for it, and she refused to sign the papers because she didn't want to sell or even lease the hotel. So she cried and cried and Father insisted that she sign the papers. Finally she did. Mother was really very involved in the hotel. She was looking over all of the people that worked in the kitchen and just really enjoyed being the top person.

MENDI: Father had let out the hotel and we had quite a nice income from that money.

EDITH: Because Mother was so unhappy about leaving the hotel, Father found a very beautiful home for us to live in. It looked like a castle. He took her there to the new house and just left her there so she wouldn't be a witness to the packing up of our belongings from the hotel, the moving. But then it seemed like Mother was never happier. When she saw where we moved, she adjusted and was happy. It looked like a mansion. We had luxurious pure leather furniture and a smoking section in the new home. We still lived in Sighet, and we were next door to Father's cousin, David Festinger.

I want to tell you about those wonderful Festinger relatives that lived in the house next door to us. David Festinger, Father's first cousin, was widowed. He was a darling, a doll! He had a nice little moustache and was always so elegantly dressed, and always busy. He had a brush factory. I called him Festinger Baci, Uncle Festinger, and he had four children there with no mother. The oldest girl, Gizi, ran the house and took care of the others. They lost their mother at a very early age. There was one boy, Milu, who later became known as Sandy. There was Betty, her real name was Bichu, and she was two years older than me. Betty wasn't my age and in those days it meant a lot. So Betty was more like my sister Hilda's friend. Betty was very wild, and she was very exciting to live next door to because she always did something bad. She got kicked out of school so many times until the end of it, when they wouldn't let her come back anymore. And every time I went outside I could hear Festinger Baci yelling at Betty and running after her while she ran away from him! There were always people screaming there. The other daughter there was Janka, who was my sister Piri's friend; they were the same age. Janka was a seamstress and she was a good girl, very lovely and so was her sister Gizi, who was really the head of the family. Their home had four or five bedrooms; it was a big white house that was fabulous. And our house was even bigger, it was gigantic. We were still a big family living there with my parents, Johnny, Pirike, Hilda, and me. I slept in a bedroom with Pirike. In the wintertime, at night we all took a hot brick, one that had been heated in the fireplace into our beds to keep us warm. Mendi was away at boarding school in Timisoara.

MENDI: Starting in 1936 I boarded at the Jewish school in Timisoara. During that time, I had another three years of school to complete. Timisoara was four hundred to five hundred kilometers from Satu-Mare, where we later moved. I liked animals and I thought I would follow agricultural studies, but then the war broke out. I would have gone to university. There were schools that accepted Jews, only a few excluded Jews. The University of Cluj accepted Jews.

EDITH: My brother Mendi was so educated. As soon as he was old enough to read novels, he discovered Zane Grey and he read all of his novels that had been translated into Hungarian. Mendi went to the Liceul Commerciale High School in Timisoara.

MENDI: I played soccer at school. I followed the First Division teams of Romania. I was a member of the Betar Zionist Youth Movement.

EDITH: I belonged to the girls Zionist group, the Shomer Hatzair. My brothers, Johnny and Mendi, were active in the boys group, the Betar. Johnny sang the Betar song in Yiddish. This is how I translate the Betar song into English: Betar Betar, Betar Hoorah! Forever loyal to you... LaLaLa…LaLaLa.

And then the Shomer Hatzair, the girls, made up cursing songs about the boys. There was so much going on there. These Zionist youth groups became the underground, when it became imperative to find ways out of Europe for the Jews.

I always went to the market place in Sighet with Mother. That was something splendid. It was open air, and very familiar to what you see anywhere at a farmer's market, but bigger, much more populated. The people that came in from other places slept there the whole night before. They were Romanian peasants and they brought wagons with them big enough for their entire families to sleep in. They always brought their whole families along to the market. The market consisted of vegetables and live poultry; usually they made a spread, like they were roasting chestnuts and cooking corn that was for sale. Beautifully hand made embroidered Romanian blouses were available to buy.

The maid came with us, to carry back all of our purchases, and I would help her. The Sighet Market was on Monday, once weekly, weather permitting. We were buying food for our family. We bought green and red cabbage, onion, beets, lettuce, carrots, potatoes, and parsley. We would walk over to the poultry and Mother would pick up the chicken and feel its tushy and put her finger on it to feel for the fat. She wanted to make sure that the chicken was nice and fat, because that gives you good chicken soup and we also needed the fat to make schmaltz for cooking and grevins. She would buy two chickens; that would have been enough for the family because we didn't eat meat everyday. We had our own chickens at home but we kept those for the eggs mostly and so we bought more chickens at the market for cooking. I helped her carry them and then we took the live poultry to the kosher butcher, and he slaughtered the poultry for us.

Because we didn't go to market in wintertime, we prepared ahead and put the foodstuff in the cellar. The potatoes we put in the dirt; that would keep them good for the winter. We were canning raspberries and raspberry syrup because we had real seltzer water to mix with it. And raspberry and strawberry jam, too. Mother made lots of giant jars of tomatoes, sauce, and juice because she was cooking with it. We made lots and lots of pickles out of the cucumbers that grew in the garden. We had the apples and the nuts for the winter, too. We made sour cabbage canned in bushels, like sauerkraut. Actually, I don't think my mother did the labor; she taught the maids how to do it and oversaw them. I never had any duties in the house, in Sighet, because a girl like me had to go to school and house duties belonged to the maids.

There were many small groceries and all types of other stores in Sighet. Sighet was an enlightened community because of European and Italian influence. The shops reflected all the modern trends. The grocery was where we bought mamaliga/pulishka, which was the most important staple. It was the corn meal, which we used a lot; in bad times we even had it for dinner. It's like polenta, and if you dry it up, it can be made into anything. As a supper, we had fried onions and schmaltz as gravy over a patty of mamaliga. We also purchased all the odds and ends that were needed in the kitchen at the groceries.

There were many trees to climb, it was fabulous. I was a good climber. I spent a lot of time up in the branches of the trees and Mother would come calling, "Lunchtime, lunchtime." So I knew that lunch was coming, that she was bringing it. I had a special basket with a thick string tied to it. I lowered the basket and Mother put my lunch in it; and I would pull it up in the tree and eat my lunch up there, which consisted of stuffed kishke made from chicken, which was made a lot. They cut from the chicken's head past the neck, cut that skin out, and sewed it up with a needle and stuffed that up real delicious and then sliced it and made sandwiches out of it. The stuffing was made from browned onions with schmaltz and garlic added to challah bread that had been soaked in eggs. Then the whole thing was baked in the oven and then I had an apple for dessert, right from the tree. I used to take that to school too. We had about eight walnut trees, but those walnuts fell on the ground and my brother Johnny made a lot of money with that, and he wouldn't give me any of that money, even for a movie! And I was working so hard for him picking up those walnuts, but I had a lot of fun doing that. There were two bedrooms in our house that no one used, so Johnny stored the apples in one and the nuts in the other. He was always a doer, like with agricultural stuff.

The older cousins and my sister didn't exclude me from anything, but I just didn't care to be with them. I had my own friends. I remember being aggravated with the cousins because they were stealing our walnuts from our trees. I didn't realize that when you have a tree and the branches are on the neighbor's property, then those branches don't belong to you anymore. So they were allowed to take the walnuts but you know how children are. The adults didn't really mix because our family was more religious and so didn't interact much; it was just the children that were together. I think we lived there three or four years. We lived at the hotel longer than we lived in that house. I know that because my memories of the hotel are stronger than my memories of that house. But in that house there was a lot of laughter, always.

The holidays were unforgettable, especially Passover. The synagogue in Sighet was very old fashioned. I think that if you travel to Israel and you see the synagogues there, you see that they are similar to the Sighet Synagogue.[7] I always went with Mother; I walked with her on the street. She wore a scarf. Later on I cried for that scarf. Aranka ended up getting that scarf and then it was lost. I loved the time alone with Mother. I was always alone with her when we went to Shule, when we were walking there, and walking home from there. And on Saturday, the Sabbath, I would sit with her in the living room.

And during that time Mendi was away at school I missed my brother very much. When he was home for the holidays I was always waiting for him. He befriended my girlfriends, and there was more than one that fell in love with my handsome brother.

MENDI: At school, I went to synagogue every Friday night and Saturday morning and occasionally during the week. I always came home from boarding school for Jewish holidays. We had a beautiful Jewish home and we observed all the holidays. My father went to synagogue every morning and every evening.

EDITH: In Sighet, I went to public school until the age of ten. At school, drawing and music theory were required courses which I truly enjoyed. One time my school had a concert that I was singing in. It was a big concert on a stage and it was the first time that we were singing. At eleven, I already went into high school for one year and then at that time we wore uniforms. We wore berets, navy berets with a silver band. And if you were in a lower grade it was a wider band. When you were promoted to a higher grade, then the silver band became thinner. Up on top it said, LDE, the name of the school was Liceul Domenica Elena, and this meant a younger girl. I belonged to a cheerleading group for the soccer team. We were doing gymnastic dance routines. Half of the team dressed as peasant girls and half of the team dressed as boys. I was on the boys' side and we wore all white cotton shirts and white cotton pants with a big black leather belt tied in front. Our black shoes were handmade with long black cotton laces that tied from the ankle up to right below the knee, like the clothing of our Roman ancestors. We wore a cone-shaped fur hat called a Kuzma.

In 1935, we had decided to move to Satu-Mare. My sister Ceca, her husband, and her little daughter were living there and she was begging my parents to join them. We were to get a big house to all live together in.

Packing up to move from Sighet to Satu-Mare was exciting. For a young girl, any kind of moving is an excitement because it's getting to know new places. By the time that they put all the furniture on a railroad car and we went, it was just pure excitement. We took bread and grapes with us to eat on the way. We just said goodbye to our cousins, and that was it.

I had gone to my first year of high school in Sighet, and we had moved a few weeks before the school year ended. I didn't finish that year's studies, so I went back to Sighet for a few weeks in the summer to finish up my exams. I stayed with the Festinger cousins for that time. Later, they came to visit in Satu-Mare.

I think it was the first summer in Satu-Mare when the Gypsies parked themselves in our backyard, because Father let them. He collected some rent from them. They stayed the whole summer. They put up their tents to house all their children. There were about ten, eleven children. They were back there making bricks. I don't know who they were making the bricks for but I remember it was a hot summer. The way that they made those bricks was interesting: they were using water and some sort of mixture and putting that into wooden forms that they put in stands on the grass. And they baked the bricks right there in the sun. I played with the Gypsy kids. I was in my first year of high school but still a kid at eleven years old.

After moving to Satu-Mare I went to an all girls' Catholic School. There were no Jewish schools for me to go to. I went to Catholic school for four years in Satu-Mare. Hilda got expelled from school because she had gone to this dancing place where young girls went. She went there without a chaperone. My brother Johnny told on her. The head master was Papa Laurence. We had school on Saturday, and because that day is Shabbos, I wasn't allowed to carry my books or do any writing. So a maid carried my books for me back and forth to school. Once weekly a Hebrew teacher would come in for the Jewish students, so we would be sure to get our religious education. Only one of the nuns there was anti-Semitic, and she was my math teacher. One time I had made a mistake in algebra and she said, "You did that because you are Jewish." Papa Laurence was having sex with some of the nuns; it was the gossip there. We had an ice skating rink at school and skating was required. Physical education was a big part of the school philosophy. The nuns skated too, and their habits were flying in the wind. That was something to see! One winter I had spots on my lungs and Mother came to school with me to get me excused from gym, so for a while I didn't ice skate.

KURT: In 1936 I took a paid vacation to Holland. I saw a lot of countries. My boss Jules and his wife Helen were good friends, and had given me the address of Helen's parents in Romania. I went there to visit and met the Festinger family and especially their daughter Piri, who was very good looking and twenty years old. It was love at first sight. After a week, we were engaged. I could not stay longer because I had a return ticket to Indonesia and had to meet the boat at Naples, Italy.

EDITH: My sister Piri had been in love with Hans, and he was a Polish Jew. He was a gorgeous, handsome boy who wore a fur coat. When Jules de Leeuw wrote to Father that Kurt Meyers was coming to meet Piri, there was a shadduch and then Piri was ordered to break up with Hans. She went to bed and was hysterical. I don't know how long she cried but she was broken hearted. I was very worried about Piri at that time, because I had never seen her so unhappy. Remember, she was always laughing and dancing. In those days she was even jumping up on the table to dance when the record player or the radio was playing all the music that was popular at the time.

One time, Kurt wanted to be alone with Piri and Hilda wouldn't leave the room. She just refused to leave. Then Pirike fell in love with Kurt, and it was very exciting for her to have the plans for moving to Indonesia. At first it was a beautiful life, she had five maids to take care of her needs.

KURT: After arriving back in Indonesia, I sent money to Piri for her trip to Indonesia. In May 1937 she arrived in Bandung. On June 2, 1937 we got married.

Piri and I traveled all over with my chauffeur to Surabaia and further by boat to Macasser, the Capital of the island of Celebes where we established our home. In 1939, I brought my mother and sister to Java, where Piri and I were then living. My daughter

Yvonne was born in Bandung and Bernard was born on a small island near Borneo.

EDITH: Micki Meyer, Ceca's husband, had also worked for Jules de Leeuw in Java. Jules had his eyes on all the Festinger girls for his friends. If there hadn't been the war, Hilda and I were next to be matched up with Jules' friends. Most of them were his employees. I remember that he tried to break up Aranka and her husband. My sister Aranka had married Eugene Schwartz on her own, although Eugene was connected to that group of people, being Micki Meyers' cousin.

There was a Jewish hospital on our street, Attila Street. I wanted to work there, to become a nurse and perhaps from there go on to become a physician. I begged Father to allow me to go into the nursing school but he refused to allow it. He said that Jewish girls did not become nurses; it was not proper. I was heartbroken. I had to give up my dream of studying medicine.

In 1939 I became a nanny in Budapest for a family of wealthy Jews. I took the train to Budapest. After a short time, my sister Hilda came to visit, and stayed with me in the city. Budapest was very contemporary with a modern transportation system. The home where I lived and worked was walking distance to the Budapest cafes and shops.

The child that I cared for was a beautiful, delicate little girl that couldn't walk and was in a wheelchair. I think she had polio. Her name was Lilli. I became very attached to her. The people were high class and the home was exquisite. They did a lot of entertaining and I was introduced as Lilli's Nanny, from

Satu-Mare. They told everyone that I had five sisters and a brother living in Java that were millionaires, dealing in diamonds. I slept in Lilli's bedroom with her, and next to my bed was a button that rang a bell into the kitchen. If I needed anything, I was to simply call for service. I spent the entire day with Lilli; she was completely under my care. I told her fairy tales and many stories that I made up especially for her. Hilda had her own private bedroom.

While in Budapest, I wanted to look up Laci Remete, a college student who was related to my family somehow. His mother, a widow, was very good friends with my sisters Helenke and Zsenka. My sisters always visited the Remete home whenever in Budapest.

One morning Laci Remete came by the home to meet me and he first passed by my bedroom window. I was wearing a beautiful, colorful bathrobe that my sisters had sent me from India. I had beautiful clothes from them: shorts, blouses, shoes; a complete wardrobe. Laci told me that when he saw me for the first time, in that robe, with my long black hair, that he thought he was dreaming. And he told me that he had fallen in love with me at that moment. I liked him a lot but I wasn't in love. Laci told me that he wanted to marry me. I spent my days off with Laci Remete.

MENDI: Edith was working in Budapest as a nanny, and Hilda had gone with her. Katzender, the family friend, who was in love with my sister Edith, had intervened, telling Father that the Russians were bombing Budapest, and that Jonas should bring the girls home.

EDITH: One day in 1939, Father's friend Katzender told him that the Russians were going to be invading Budapest and bombing the city and Father made us come back home.

Laci Remete was very dramatic and told me that I didn't love him or I would have stayed. The little girl cried a lot when we said good-bye. I had a big fight with little Lili's mother because she accused me of being ungrateful, and after all she had done for me. She said that because she let Hilda stay there, I should be grateful. I told her, "I learned back home that once you throw up a good deed, then it is not a good deed anymore." And so we returned to Satu-Mare.

In Satu-Mare, the downtown was still a bustling social scene. It was customary that families sat down for dinner at six o'clock. As soon as the dinner clean up was completed, all of the families headed for the boardwalk, where people walked up and down, a lot with baby strollers. It was close to the market. All along the boardwalk there were vendors who used little stoves and sold their roasted chestnuts and roasted sweet potatoes. There was a music gazebo for bands, a famous hotel, and taxi drivers parked in front of it.

Sometimes Hilda and I would jump on a local bus to get there, as the bus driver was Jewish he would let us girls ride for free. We were eager to get to the boardwalk, as we always knew the boys would be there! It was a big coquetry, you know, we were flirting with the boys. This is how it worked: the eyes would seek out a match, and when the eye contact happened with the right partner, it was magic. You just knew who was right!

There were local photographers and they knew who everyone was, and that we would be out on the boardwalk. They took our photos and developed them and the next day would show up at our homes, offering the photos for sale.

Katzender was always on the Satu-Mare boardwalk and that is where he first saw me, and then was always looking at me.

MENDI: It was 1939, and we absolutely didn't feel any change. Until the Hungarians came in, and then we started to worry. Father was desperate to save my brother John from being drafted into the Hungarian Army, and when the war broke out he then sold the Tisza Hotel in Sighet for a fraction of the price that it was worth. He used all of that money in order to send my bother to Indonesia; he bribed officials to get a passport for him. I remember that it cost 150,000 Lei. We had gotten 350,000 Lei for the hotel and he sent John by train to Italy, to try to get a ship there, but the Italians sent John back from the border. They wouldn't let him through. So, he came back and Father got him on an airplane and all the money went on him. Johnny was saved from being taken into the Hungarian Army and Father probably saved his life that way. He got to Indonesia although he didn't have a permit to get in. The war had broken out over there and they couldn't send him anywhere.

EDITH: My sister Helen, her husband Jules de Leeuw, and their two children had embarked on a world trip in early 1939. They attended the World's Fair in New York City and bought a car there, which they brought with them to Europe and then traveled by car when they came to visit Satu-Mare. Then the war broke out and they had to leave the car behind. They took a plane back to Indonesia and then moved to Sydney, Australia, ahead of the Japanese invasion.

MENDI: I had been in a labor force for three months. I had a bad arm, so they didn't take me into the army. I had to go for three months to Cluj, into the labor force. We had to repair wheat bags; that was part of it. Then another time we mined sand, it wasn't hard, and then they sent us back home. Because we were handicapped, they only took us for three months; otherwise we would have had to serve perhaps on the Russian front. A lot of friends did and most of them died there.[8]

EDITH: The day the Hungarians marched in, in 1940, was a joyful, moving experience. There was a marching band playing in Satu-Mare. Soldiers were marching and Father was so happy. You see, he preferred the Hungarians and was not happy with Romanian control. Little did he know what a tragedy it would bring because the Hungarians became one with the Germans. The Romanians did not.

I met a Hungarian soldier who was not Jewish. He fell in love with me and wrote a letter to me proposing marriage. I snuck out to meet him and we were walking in the park. As I went to touch the collar of his jacket, I discovered an SS Gestapo button hidden under that collar. That was a sure sign that he was a Nazi. I was shocked and told him that my father would rather find me dead. I ran home and tried to forget this.

My real boyfriend was Jani Braun. We spent a lot of time climbing in the mountains, just walking and hiking. One beautiful day he took a pocketknife out and carved our names on a rock. Jani lived in Nagybana and once I took a bus there to visit him; it took a few hours to get there. I was there for three days, and stayed with Mother's brother, who had a farm there. I had met Jani in Satu-Mare, which was where he went for high school. I used to watch him walk by my house every day in Satu-Mare. He was eighteen and I was sixteen when we first met.

KURT: On December 7, 1941, the day Pearl Harbor was bombed, Holland was also at war with Japan. I was immediately drafted into the Dutch Indonesian Army. Piri, our children, my mother, my sister, and the rest of the Festinger family were on their own.

MENDI: After 1941 we were affected financially because the money from Indonesia did not come. So for a while it was quite difficult. Then one day my father came home and he said that a Christian friend of his had started with Angora rabbits and he wanted me to come and have a look at it. I always loved animals. We started to breed rabbits and my sister Edith learned to spin wool. And she taught me to spin, too.

EDITH: Our Angora rabbit farm was a real illustration of human adaptation during wartime. The world was upside-down, and the rabbit farm enabled my brother and me to completely support our family during those times, from 1942 until 1943. The rabbit farm was located at our house on Attila Street, in Satu-Mare. My brother Mendi knew a lot about animals, he had been ready to go to college to be a veterinarian.

During this time in our country the economic situation was absolutely treacherous. Because we were Jewish, there were few opportunities to earn money. Just the fact that we were Jewish cut all the businesses down and up to that point we were starving along with the rest of the Jewish people.

The rabbit farm provided an income for my family since our parents had no way to support all of us. Mendi had two thousand Angora rabbits of different colors, which he raised and crossbred. The house had a large terrace off the back, completely enclosed with doors and windows, so in the wintertime it wasn't so cold, and in the summertime the screens kept the insects out of the cages. Each cage was quite big, giving the rabbits plenty of room. When the mother was ready to deliver the baby rabbits somebody had to stay and watch, twenty-four hours, because if they didn't have enough water, they would chew on the little babies' legs or start eating parts and they became cannibals. When the baby rabbits were just old enough so that the hair was the right length, Mendi sheared the hair very precisely with scissors. We had shoeboxes ready to lay the hair in. Then the rabbits were bald, just like lambs! The hair would start growing back on the rabbits right away. We had a very large house and I was set up in another section. I had a spinning wheel, which were common in Romania. I sat in a chair in a certain position with the spinning wheel in front of me. It had to be between my knees. There was a place where the yarn came out spinning into a ball. The hair was lying on a towel in my lap. With the palms of my two hands, I kept feeding the machine, just the proper amount to make the exact perfect thread. It was like holding a very gentle bird in your hands. As I held the hair and fed it into the machine, it became like a kaleidoscope. It was fascination; the fact that I was feeding the hair into the machine and it came out as yarn. There was a foot pedal and one of my feet was pedaling, pumping the wheel so it would move. Then as the amount of thread, or yarn became big enough, I stopped. Then, since this wasn't a factory, someone helped me by holding out their two hands and I was winding the yarn around to make a skein. I didn't have to weigh it, I knew by feeling; by intuition.

Here is something very funny: My neighbor had a dog. I told her, "Give me the hair that comes off of your dog, and I will make you a little yarn." And I did!

Even though I was terribly young, I learned to spin real fast and before long I was spinning so fast that you could hardly see my fingers, they were going like a fan. In all of Satu-Mare County that I was in, it was known that there was not another person equal to me in my knowledge of spinning. In fact, the local teacher of this craft, the one who had taught me, came back to me and asked me to teach her how to spin! Mendi knew how to spin too, but he wasn't as fast as I was.

Mendi's expertise was with the animals. Although he was very young, he had gained that knowledge of animals when he went to private school. Then, by himself, he learned how to make medications for the ailing rabbits. He actually healed them with concoctions that he mixed. So Mendi took care of the animals. The spinning, dyeing of the yarn, knitting, and selling were my responsibility. I was making these skeins one after another and after that they were sent to a certain company that was associated with the dry cleaners in town, to be dyed in different colors. Then I hired ten to fourteen girls to work for me. I knew these girls; they were city girls, not peasants. They knitted in their homes. They helped me, and I also knew how to knit everything. I was a leader, and I told them what I wanted: boleros, jackets, sweaters, and dresses. These items were sold locally, or I went up to Budapest, the capital of Hungary and sold them to very exclusive stores.

MENDI: We made a good living. We gave out the wool to girls to knit jumpers, cardigans, and my two younger sisters went to Budapest with the garments and sold them very easily. Even Mother used to knit. She knitted very nicely and we made a good living from that.

EDITH: When I traveled to Budapest, my older sister Hilda went with me. It was absolutely forbidden, in that society, for a girl to travel alone. I knew where to go to sell the garments because several of these exclusive shop owners in Budapest had already heard about us. My garments were stylish and very expensive. They paid cash, in the Romanian Lei. We did quite well.

At one very elegant store in Budapest, where we went into carrying a box with two or three colorful Angora sweaters, I needed to prove something, because I could see at the present time that what we Jews were experiencing didn't affect other people. This shopkeeper was looking at my sweaters, especially a jade green one, and didn't even seem surprised or in a state of awe that those gorgeous colored sweaters held historical significance! I asked him if he knew what was going on here and he refused to comprehend our story. I told him that our family had an Angora rabbit farm and other Jewish people were struggling, adapting, doing what we had to in order to make a living. He was absolutely nonchalant about all of it. I found that odd.

We stayed with the Remete's in Budapest. It was so good to see Laci Remete again. We spent two nights at their place. I didn't realize how much I cared for Laci, and he was still in love with me. But we had to get back home. We had the Angora business to attend to, and it wasn't a good idea for young women to be running around, during those shaky times.

Back in Satu-Mare, the word had spread, and people were begging me to spin for them. One in particular was an artist, a famous man, who was a friend of Father's who had a few Angora rabbits. He asked me to spin for him, so I did it as a favor. He paid me very well.

It wasn't normal for girls or children to work in my country. It just wasn't natural. But to do what I did, on my own at home, was accepted. The main thing is that we lived well and that was very satisfying.

I want to tell you what else I did during that time. I stayed up until four o'clock in the morning, painting watercolor paintings and I sold those too. I always wonder where my paintings are, where they ended up. To this day, I cannot pick up a paintbrush. It is just too painful.

KURT: In March of 1942 all of us in the Dutch army surrendered to the Japanese. I became a prisoner of war. It was hard labor and beatings for us, and the Japanese moved us about every six months to different places. The food was terrible and many friends died from berry berry or dysentery and other sicknesses.

EDITH: My sister Piri never talked about the two and a half years they were in the Japanese camps. The only thing she told me was that when the women and children were moved from camp to camp, each time, Piri had to carry her mother-in-law's mattress on her back. And Kurt's sister was mentally handicapped. So Piri cared for all of them during that awful time.

MENDI: In 1942 quite a few Polish Jews came to our area with false papers saying that they were Christians. They were telling us stories and we wouldn't believe it.

EDITH: In 1943, Grandfather was eighty-seven and had passed away naturally. He was laid out in the main dining room of our home in Satu-Mare. It was the day before we would bury him. We were getting ready for the services to lay him to rest in the cemetery.

I was waiting for a letter from Jani Braun; my boyfriend was in jail then. Jani was in trouble; he had been arrested for working for the Jewish underground, distributing leaflets. The local Zionist boys, the Betar, were teamed up with the Israelies. The Israeli guys went to all of the European countries trying to get the Jews out. Somehow Jani was allowed to write to me and I was writing to him. I lived for his letters, we were in love. The postman would put the mail through a slot in the window that was in that room. I had to run through there to get my letter and Grandfather's body was there. I had to do it because my Jani's letter was waiting for me.

There was a tragic, tragic day when I don't know how, but Father went to buy the yellow stars that we had to sew on our clothes. I went downtown with my sister Hilda and I heard the guys with the girls on their arms singing a song, "...Tomorrow night the Jewish star will be in the sky, the yellow star, and the Jews will be in the sky..." And I don't know how Father got all of us to sew those stars on all our clothes. It's an amazing thing that happens to a young girl when tragedy comes around. They don't take things as tragic as it should be. Everything to them is an exciting movement. Do you realize that? That is what happens. Like I had all of these ideas, that I am not going to be alone there, there will be other people there and maybe I would see some nice boys there. Because nothing had really happened yet; we didn't know what we were going into.

One day, in Satu-Mare, about six weeks before we were forced into the Ghetto, and after the rabbits had been sold; I was walking on Attila Street with my girlfriend, Sidi Riderman. Sidi was my best girlfriend. Originally she was Hilda's friend, and then we got to know each other. We had a lot in common after high school, and always had so much to talk about. I spent many nights staying overnight at her home. This day, as we were walking and talking, we heard the sound of boots behind us, following us. Two men were behind us; they were German soldiers. I heard one say to the other, "Shana madel." Sidi and I grabbed each other's hands and we started running and then we turned into a side street where we approached her home and ran inside. Sidi told her mother that two soldiers were behind us, following us. Sidi's mother yelled, "Go upstairs to the attic, run!" We went all the way up to the attic and we were shaking and sobbing, scared to death, and they were coming right behind us. Then we heard Sidi's mother, she had run into the street and was screaming to two German officers that also were out there. She said to them, "Two of your soldiers are attacking my daughter and her friend!" She had a tavern attached to the house and when she ran into the tavern; the German officers followed her in. There happened to be a couple of chickens and a goose inside, right in the hallway. And the German officers were laughing and saying in German, "Look at the chickens." The other two soldiers were only one step away from entering the attic and now there were four Germans inside the house. The officers yelled at the two soldiers to get outside and go to the station, or else they would be punished. They did not know that we were Jewish. If they had known that we were, it would have been another story. After that I

56

ran home and when I reached the inside of my house, I broke down sobbing hysterically.

Then when the Germans came and started taking the Jews away, Father's Christian friend, the artist, offered to hide me in his home, so I would not be sent to prison camp. I would not even consider leaving my family.

Jonas and Regina Festinger, Sighet early 1920's

Ceca Festinger, Sighet early 1920's

Helen Festinger, Sighet 1928

Johnny Festinger, Romanian Cavalry 1932

Mendi Festinger, Timisoara 1936

Hilda (left) and Edith (right), Satu-Mare Boardwalk 1938

Edith Festinger, Satu-Mare Market 1939

Edith Festinger, Lake Nagybana 1940

Part 2

Chapter Three

The Final Solution with regard to Hungary was carried out, and with the help of the Hungarians the Nazis implemented the solution of the Hungarian Jews at 'lightning speed' under Obersturmbannfuhrer Adolf Eichmann. In Satu-Mare on April 6, 1944 the first conference on the dejewification operations was held.[9] The second conference was held April 8 in Targu-Mare. The Ghettoization Drive of approximately 160,000 Jews from Northern Transylvania began... " By Decree no. 6163/1944, that stipulated that the Jews would be concentrated in empty warehouses, factories, brickyards, and the Jewish community establishments, schools, offices, and synagogues. These Ghettos were to be near adequate rail facilities to make possible swift entrainment and deportation...time was of the essence...the fast approach of the Red Army..." Because of the large amount of Jews in Satu-Mare County, two ghettos were set up, one in Satu-Mare which held approximately 18,000 and the other one in Baia-Mare. A small commando of about 100 SS men accomplished the mission with the total support of the newly established Hungarian government. "The Jews were rounded up with great speed, given only a few minutes to pack, and driven into the ghettos on foot..."[10] The ghettoization drive in Northern Transylvania was completed within one week.

Edith Festinger and her family were ordered to take only what they could carry on their backs and driven into the streets, along with the other Jews of Satu-Mare, with the Hungarian people cheering the Nazis on.

After a few weeks in the Satu-Mare Ghetto the Festingers and all the others were herded to the railroad, where they were to travel to their destination—Auschwitz, the infamous death camp set up to exterminate millions of Jewish people. In less than three months, the Hungarian police, in coordination with the Germans, deported nearly 440,000 Jews from all of the ghettos in Hungary. Most were sent to the Auschwitz-Birkenau killing center.[11] Dejewification of the Satu-Mare ghetto went on schedule. The liquidation and the deportation of these Jews were accomplished in six railway transports between May 19 and June 1, 1944:

1. May 19   3,006 deportees

2. May 22   3,300 deportees

3. May 26   3,336 deportees

4. May 29   3,306 deportees

5. May 30   3,300 deportees

6. June 1   2,615 deportees

Regina and Jonas Festinger, Ceca Festinger and her husband Micki Meyer, and their thirteen-year-old daughter Greta, were murdered in Auschwitz on June 2, 1944.

On June 6, 1944, D-Day, the Invasion of Normandy was begun by the Western Allies to liberate the continent of Europe from Nazi occupation. After almost two years of planning, this would prove to be a turning point in World War II, although it did not alter the cataclysmic events for the Festinger family until almost a year later.

Nathan Litvin was among the 154,000 Allied troops who safely entered the coast of Normandy and initiated the retreat of the Nazis. The D-Day attack was the largest amphibious assault ever attempted and was code-named Operation Overlord. Nate landed at Utah Beach as part of the United States Army amphibian task force.

Nathan (Nate) Litvin was born in Detroit, Michigan on January 14, 1921 to Baruch (Boris) and Ida Litvin (both born circa 1890), Russian immigrants who had fled the pogroms. Baruch Litvin was born in the tiny village of Makarov, of five to eight houses.[12] Nate's grandfather had a few cows and made butter and cheese. Nate's mother was Ida Reizen, whose father was in the Russian army, his job going to Afghanistan to bring horses back to Kiev. The Litvin/Lettvin clan can be traced back to the mid 1300s.[13] Around the age of thirteen, Baruch Litvin became a political radical. He was arrested and sent to Siberia where he shared a jail cell with Lenin and Trotsky. Baruch escaped and returned home to Makarov, where his mother, Gittel Lettvin hid him from the police. After that, Baruch went to Kiev, and met a Jewish man in the glass business that later gave him the money to emigrate to New York. In 1906, Baruch Litvin left Russia on the Carpathia (his age listed on the ship's manifest as 18).[14] He departed from Trieste.[15] From New York, Baruch went to Chicago, where he sold newspapers, then became a barber.[16] He financed the immigration of his large Russian family to America. During World War I Baruch was a carpenter on large office buildings in Chicago. Baruch and Ida Litvin had four sons. Paul and Morris (Moe) were born in Chicago and then the family moved to Detroit for 'great opportunity' and had two more sons, Nathan (Nate) and Emanuel (Manny). Baruch opened a successful window manufacturing business and became the first to sell windows with the glass prior to being installed in the homes. Baruch and Ida sent their eldest son Paul to the Mikveh Israel agricultural boarding school in Israel, to keep him out of the Purple Gang.[17]

During the depression, Baruch Litvin bought a thirty-one-acre farm in Davis, Michigan and started a chicken business, selling eggs. Nate Litvin grew up a strong farm boy, tending the chickens, collecting the eggs and selling them on a route, and milking and feeding the cows with his brother Manny. The boys' chores included tending twenty fruit trees consisting of plum, apple, and apricot, and growing vegetables for sale. There was a tractor on the farm, which the boys drove and maintained. They went to the two-room Davis School through eighth grade and also to private Hebrew school lessons to prepare for their Bar Mitzvahs. By 1935, the chicken business failed and Baruch decided to get back into the lumber *business and purchased Paganetti Lumber Company in Mount Clemens, Michigan.*

At Mount Clemens High School, Nate was a natural athlete, and became a champion boxer, football player, and a member of the wrestling team. He loved to compete, and was an award-winning member of the debate team.[18] In his third year he was awarded a letter for football. In his senior year, as Captain of the football team, The Battling Bathers (named for the city's famous mineral baths), he led the Mount Clemens team undefeated to become champions of the Border Cities League.[19] Nate Litvin graduated from Mount Clemens High School in 1939. In his high school yearbook, the Clemensian, he was described, as 'A ruddy drop of manly blood.' In 1941-1942 Nate was Captain of the City Champions basketball team in Mount Clemens.[20] Nathan Litvin had been a college student attending Wayne State University, in Detroit, Michigan when he was drafted into the U.S. Army. He was planning on finishing college and becoming a veterinarian.

☙

NATE: I had been drafted into the Army and inducted on August 11, 1942. I had said goodbye to my parents and grandparents in Chicago, Illinois where they saw me off.

I went to basic training at Fort Wheeler in Macon, Georgia. I got qualified in rifle marksmanship. I shipped out to Europe in January of '42. I was in the infantry. I was one of more than 23,000 American troops that had landed at Utah Beach on D-Day, June 6, 1944. My unit was the 363rd Quartermaster Service Company. After the invasion, my job was on the team that recovered the dead soldiers' bodies on Utah Beach.

MENDI: The Germans had marched into Satu-Mare in the Spring of 1944. Then, after a week or two, the Germans told us we had to go into a ghetto. They cordoned off a few streets where actually a lot of Jews used to live. We could take with us whatever we could carry and we went in, into the ghetto.

EDITH: My love for Jani Braun was all consuming. He was my boyfriend. He had written to me, around twenty-five letters altogether. I had wrapped these letters in a blue ribbon. They were my strength and my hope to carry on for the future. The letters would be there to put a smile on my face.

I felt no pain and I felt no tears dripping down my face, as I was dead tired walking to the ghetto, I could feel Jani's hand upon my waist. I imagined his kiss upon my lips and my eyes were searching for him. He was nowhere to be seen and suddenly I knew that I would never see Jani again. Later on when the Nazi grabbed my bag away from me, I knew in that instant that Jani was dead.

MENDI: We all had to sleep in one small room. It was my parents, Edith and Hilda, my sister Ceca with her husband Micki, and their daughter Greta. We had our bedding with us. We took quite a lot of food with us. We had enough food while we were in the ghetto. I think we were there two or three weeks. There was one German officer, who was in charge of the ghetto.

EDITH: In the last days of the ghetto, Father shaved his beard off. He did that because of the harassment that he was suffering. I almost did not recognize him, when I first saw him without his beard.

On one of those days, I was out on the cordoned off streets and happened to look up at another building. In a window on the top floor, I saw my cousin Gizi Festinger staring out of the window. She was holding her baby.

Then Ceca went out and bought a ham, so we would have food that would not spoil. And Father did not say anything.

MENDI: The same German officer, who was in charge of the ghetto, took us to the train. We didn't know where we were being taken. They told us they were taking us to farms. We were to have work on the farms; that was what they said.

EDITH: Now, when I look back, I see how happy I was, being yet together with my family. My happiness ended after that. We got an order to be ready to go to the railroad. The SS soldiers put all of us humans in a small train wagon. We were on the way for about three days.

In that moment that the Germans governed us in Hungary, my personality wasn't important anymore. I did know that my life was finished. The only thing that made me worried was my mother. On the way to Auschwitz I could not give Mother a drink of water. Every door of the wagon was closed. Sometimes an SS soldier looking in asked us if we were thirsty. "Give me gold, if you want to drink," he said. We had no gold, so I had to see my mother how she suffered from thirst and no sleep. But it made no difference, because I felt her near me. I could say "Mother." I felt that somebody loves me. If she had to suffer, I could suffer with her and make her days easier.

MENDI: They put us in a wagon, seventy to eighty in a wagon. We just had enough room to sit down. It was cramped for space. I don't remember exactly how long it took but it was two or three days and the family was still together. I remember Father telling me, "Tell them that you can work." He must have known more than he told us. I remembered that advice later, which probably saved my life. We arrived in Auschwitz about two or three days later.

EDITH: Human beings locked in a boxcar. Destination unknown. We were told that they would imprison us somewhere in Hungary. Reason for this: the German guards were limited. Panic was a luxury they could do without. No food, water, or medication. Bathroom facility consisted of a couple of buckets. Confinement lasted for three days. Usually parents try to tranquil their children. Not in this case. They seemed petrified, numb, and listless. The pain I felt watching my parents is impossible to relay.

Lately in the news media some people, the Holocaust deniers, claim that pictures taken of the infamous camps were propaganda. Here is one living soul that lived to experience and was spared to shout loud enough to wake God. Everything you see is true and so much more to tell that it would give you nightmares. I was a young girl of twenty, but my mind was that of one hundred years old. Mama, Papa how I wish I could forget for one day at least. Impossible.

After travel of about three days we arrived at a large camp. We could see a great fire, which made me feel very strange. I did not know what it was. The people had great fear; they wept and prayed to God, that He would save their lives. Traveling deeper in the camp I saw four other fires; they were all crematoriums.

MENDI: When we arrived in Auschwitz we lined up in queues, men on one side, the women on the other side, and I remember a man in front of us with a little boy. An officer came to him and flicked his hat off. The officer had a walking stick and as the man bent down to pick up his hat the German officer hit him with that walking stick, so hard that he broke the stick in two. Blood was flowing from his head and I remember the little boy crying. The man was alive, but his brain must have been damaged, he was hit so hard.

My father was with me and then they sent my father to the left and they sent me to the right. And I did not see my sisters and my mother but then we were already inside the camp. A Jewish man told us he had been there for years and said, "Do you see that smoke over there coming from that big building? They are burning your parents now", and I cursed him and none of us in my group believed it. For months I hoped that my parents were still alive. You see we had seen one camp with a lot of old Jews and we were told that they were Czechoslovakian Jews.[21] So we still hoped that they kept the parents alive until much later on until I knew for sure that they were killed. You wonder why those Jews were kept alive? Obviously so we would believe that our parents were still alive. It was a trick, yes.

Regarding the selection at Auschwitz: obviously they were choosing those strongest, those that could work. They took away everything I had with me except my boots and they gave us prison garb. I was with Zalmoud Meyer, my bother-in-law Micki's youngest brother and we stayed together in Auschwitz for about two weeks. Those chosen to go to the left; my father, my mother, my sister Ceca, her husband Micki and their daughter Greta, who was about thirteen years old, they would all die there. They were the closest family members. I never saw them again. Edith and Hilda, my two younger sisters went to the right. They were in Auschwitz six or seven months.

EDITH: We got an order to step out of the train and to stand five people in a line like soldiers. I didn't let go of my mother's hand. With my other hand I caught my sister's child. Not far from us a young good looking German officer picked out all the people and children, showing them with the right hand the way to death. With the left hand he picked out the young and strong girls. The SS officer looked so human, you could not anticipate that he was the persecutor. He looked at me saying, "Swarze links to the left." I didn't want to let my mother's hand go, she was looking so sad, so unhappy, that I shall never forget. My feelings were right because from that moment on I have never seen my parents again. They had gone right to the crematorium.

Any Jewish mother that held a child's hand was sent to the left. My sister Ceca was holding little Greta's hand. The child was ripped away.

Hilda and I managed to stay together, even though they made a point of separating families. She was a blonde and I was a brunette; we didn't look like we were sisters. We waited many hours in a room where we got an order to undress ourselves. They shaved off our hair, we got a long dress without underwear: no shoes, no stockings and at last we had to march into the camp of Auschwitz, where they put us 1,200 girls in a small barrack. We were tattooed with numbers. We now were nameless, we were numbers now. For three days we didn't get anything to drink or to eat.

Every day we had to get up at two o'clock in the morning to stand like soldiers to be counted. And daily we trekked into the showers, not knowing if poison gas or water would be spraying on us. [22] The food we got in those six months was a little soup and a little black bread every day. Now I cannot understand, how we could live like that. Why didn't we take our lives?

We got some kind of medicaments in the soup— Brohm, which made us feel stupid, we couldn't think of anything. [23] We suffered six months there staying eight hours in the streets between the barracks in the rain, in the cold, and sometimes on our knees.

FROM THE REPORT FOR AMERICAN LIBERATION FORCES
AUSCHWITZ, by Edith Festinger, May 1945, in Munich, Germany

The war is over now and I am trying to describe this concentration camp called Auschwitz. The proof that I was incarcerated is obvious from the tattooed number on my forearm, which I will carry with me always. This death camp, Auschwitz, was located in Poland, which was occupied by the Germans during World War II. The city of Birkenau was not far from Auschwitz, the closest one in contact with this camp. Auschwitz itself under normal circumstances was used to keep horses. In fact, the barracks where we prisoners were kept were built for horses. The camp was divided into streets. Each street held 30,000 people. Each barrack held 1,200 women and girls, or men; which of course were separated. The roofs were leaking, the floors were muddy. Hunger and sickness soon took over the newcomers that were imported each day from their homelands. The size of this camp was enormous, wired all around with electric fence. The purpose of this was to prevent the prisoners from escaping. If they tried, they were electrocuted by the mere touch of the fence. If at any time one would recognize a relative or friend on the next street behind the electric wires, they would reach out to greet each other, unconscious of the death trap in the electrical fences. You could see the bodies hanging attached to the wires. Roll call was an everyday habit that got the prisoners out of their barracks at 2:00 A.M. At this time through the camp there was a silence, you could only hear howls of vicious dogs that the German guards kept and the cries of the sick, who were lying all over. The roll calls lasted eight hours each day, at which time no one was allowed to move, talk, or sit for any reason unless death took over. After a while, human beings soon transformed and the survival instinct cried out in them, fighting for survival. Food was little and bad. Black coffee (called ersatz) in the morning and in the evening there was soup made of a mixture that one could not possible describe. Each day the prisoners had to disrobe and a German doctor would come and look at them, selecting the sick and weak ones out. The doctor at Auschwitz was Dr. Mengele. These were sent to the gas chambers and then cremated. The gas was not always fatal, so some of these victims were thrown in the crematorium while they were still breathing. A special detail of men would come into our sections every day and pick up the dead bodies in carts. If one observed this camp from a distance, they could easily mistake it for an insane asylum, judging by the way its inhabitants looked. The women had their heads shaved completely, bare feet, and wearing nothing else but a dress given to them regardless of their sizes or shapes. The dress had a white X on the back so if they tried to escape, the guards would hit the target. People were tattooed with numbers on their arm for identification. These people—hungry, separated from their families, broken of their morale, naturally didn't care much and they acted accordingly. At night, for instance, since there weren't any accommodations, they were forced to use their eating dishes for toilet facilities. One of the barracks was used for a restroom. This 'restroom' had to accommodate 30,000 people. It had about one hundred seats in it, with holes in the ground. The people were marched into these places once or twice a day, taking turns. After about six months of this, they gave the prisoners special jobs to do, like digging ditches, cutting or breaking stones, and helping in the 'shower rooms.' The shower rooms were their specialty. They would drive the people in there, making them think that they will take baths. The ceilings of these rooms were specifically punched with little holes. As soon as they had a certain amount in one shower room, an outside man would pull a lever and let gas escape through those holes in the ceilings. Voila! Mass killings. Railroad tracks were installed all the way into the Concentration Camp. This would allow hundreds of boxcars in every day. These boxcars transported captured people from France, Poland, Hungary, Russia, Holland, Italy, Czechoslovakia, and Germany. These people traveled as long as three, four, or more days. These people were crammed in each boxcar, without food, water, or rest room facilities. But at this point, the families were still together. As soon as they reached their destination—Auschwitz—they got off the train and were separated from their families immediately. All mothers that *held a child by the hand were cremated, also all little children below the age where they could not be useful were killed. After a trial period of six months, one year, or three years, they were transported in groups deep into Germany for slave labor, mostly ammunition factories on twelve-hour shifts from 6:00 A.M. to 6:00 P.M. or 6:00 P.M. to 6:00 A.M. There was no chance to sleep with bombings continually going on until the American and Russian troops came for liberation.*

EDITH: Blokova was a Kapo, a Polish Jewish female prisoner that was put in command of 1,200 females in Auschwitz. She kept threatening, "If you don't keep silent, we'll go up in flames with our parents." Girls used the bowls that they ate in to go to the toilet. I didn't. They had one bunk transformed into toilets with hundreds of holes in it. Very often girls used to fall in them or we often used to go in there when it rained. Whatever food we had, we ate there too. The showers that they made us take were for delousing, the reason being because we all had lice.

MENDI: My youngest sister Edith got typhus and the other sister Hilda went with her into the hospital.

EDITH: In Auschwitz, very early on, we were both in the infirmary with typhus. Hilda was crying because she wanted a pair of shoes. There was a Polish nurse and she told Hilda, "Just wait, do you see that girl over there? She will die soon and then you can have her shoes." And then soon after she threw us out of there in order to save our lives. You see, the Nazis had only set up the infirmary so that they could come in and see who was dying.

I faced Hell in prison with courage; never lost self-respect or the will to live. Someone had to be sane. Helping others gave me a reason to fight. I used daydreaming and positive thinking to make believe that one day the electric fence would disappear. The eyes that are the reflecting pool of so much joy became wretched. We were souls in the palms of the Nazis hands. The tremendous power was exercised over our people, to play cruel games as if these humans were toys that didn't hear or see. And all that time I thought that maybe my parents were alive. That was one of many reasons why I fought to live.

MENDI: After about two weeks in Auschwitz, Zalmoud and I were taken in a wagon, on a train to Mauthausen. On the way from Auschwitz to Mauthausen the German officers that were with us in the wagon, they were reading the newspaper, and we could see the headline, in German, that the Allies had landed. I think it was the 6th of June 1944. Yes, and we were very happy, we thought that the war would be finished in four weeks. Unfortunately after that we had a hell of a year.

When we arrived in Mauthausen, at the station, we were lined up in fours and started marching. All the guards were Ukrainian soldiers and they started to beat us and were yelling, "Alf gain, alf gain", which means 'get on' and my friend and I were separated and I never saw him after that. We were put in different camps in Mauthausen.[24]

And then from Mauthausen, I was sent to a place called Melk, which was about one thousand kilometers east of Linz. I was on the train again.

The food was very bad in Melk. For lunch they gave us a soup made out of sugar beets, no meat in it, that was all we got for lunch. One piece of thin black bread at night, one slice of salami, one small piece of margarine, and tea, but not real tea. The food was the same in Auschwitz and in Mauthausen. We suffered a lot from hunger.

In the first few months it was still summer, but then in September it started to be cold. In October it was already very cold. I had two very good friends with me in Melk. One was Bernard. The other one was older than us, in his late forties. He had been a prisoner in Siberia for four years and he told us that it had not been so cold in Siberia as it was here in Melk. And the three of us made a pact, that if we did not get warmer clothing within four weeks, that we would kill ourselves. The older man didn't wait, he hanged himself, and about two weeks later we got warmer clothes, a jumper, plus an overcoat and underwear.

In Melk we were in previous army barracks and from there we marched to a special station made for the prisoners. I remember waiting for the train and we got on to the train and traveled over to a place, a few kilometers away to a mountain. They were building factories inside the mountain. Quite a few people killed themselves when they arrived by throwing themselves under the driving trains. So they made us sit, with our backs to the train. That way they prevented people from committing suicide. Quite a lot of people succeeded in killing themselves.

We had all come to Melk, I don't know how many, or where the others came from. There might have been 10,000 of us; all nationalities, not just Jews. There were a lot of Russian POW's, Polish, and a lot of young French. I remember I made friends with two young French brothers and they told us they were just picked off the street and brought there. And these boys were Christians. There were some Greek Jews, a lot of Yugoslavs. In fact all nationalities were there. There were many people from Satu-Mare, hundreds from my hometown, and I knew quite a lot of them.

Even though, at that time, we didn't know exactly the fate of our parents, by then I had given up all hope of seeing my parents again. Before that I remember praying for six months. I used to pray morning and night because I remembered the prayers by heart. And one day I gave up but there were still religious Jews who kept praying.

My little sisters were the lucky ones because after six months in Auschwitz they were sent to slave labor in Altenburg, Germany until the war ended.

EDITH: On what became my last day in Auschwitz, the long, narrow room filled quickly as we were pushed closely into inspection lines. A man appeared, and in our stupor we wondered if this was the Messiah. He had a long white beard, civilian attire, was very tall and had an outstretched arm. He was choosing who of us would survive death. This man was the emissary of a factory and he was making the choice between life and death; who would be sent to the Krupp Factory in Altenburg, Germany, although at that point we didn't know what or where our destination would be. The agony of the situation was deadly. About five minutes passed, but it seemed like much longer until this man pointed to those of us who were the lucky ones, and we were handed a coat and a loaf of bread. Suddenly there were screams of relief. But then, a howling of agony began, because the ones that were not chosen had the realization that there were no more coats or bread.

My eyes found my sister's eyes and silently we understood, at that moment that our destinies were to continue. We searched for others with coats and bread and six of us Jewish girls clung together, as we were herded into the same boxcar, destination Altenburg, Germany.

MENDI: In Melk I didn't have it very hard. We had two German Kapos who were previously criminal prisoners. One of them stuck a knife in one Jewish man, yet to me the Kapo was good. I had lost my shoes, actually somebody pinched them, and for a few days I walked without shoes. One of those two Kapos, he got me a pair of wooden clogs. To me they were quite good. And they didn't make me work too hard. They put me on light work like carrying water and things like that.

They were building factories inside the mountain. They started in 1944 to build factories a few stories high in order to manufacture munitions. But luckily the war ended before they could start making the munitions. I got inside the mountain. I suffered very much from the cold and one day, I think it was in January I went to the hospital and asked the doctor to put me on lighter work. I was hoping to get into the kitchen. That was the best, of course, where there was plenty of wood. He gave me a certificate to go inside the mountain and I escaped the cold. The cold and the hunger was the worst part of the concentration camp. The clothing that they had given us was not enough for being outside.

For some reason, it was warm inside; it was very warm inside the mountain. There were a few German officers but it was the Kapos that were in charge, even Jewish people as Kapos. And there were German criminals who were also in charge. Very few of those German officers mixed with us, with the exception of one or two. Yes, the Kapos were in charge. Once we arrived to work, the German companies were then in charge and we were handed over to them. We worked in shifts. There were three shifts a day, and we rotated. Sometimes I worked the day shift and sometimes in the nighttime. Once, I was two weeks on the night shift and we arrived back in the morning to sleep. I had just fallen asleep and they woke me up telling me that I had to go back to work again. They were a man short, so they took me. And that day we heard American planes. We could see flames from the camp. When we turned back I heard that at the place where I slept, eight hundred people were burned to death. The Americans threw incendiary bombs because they believed that they were hitting German barracks. I had a lucky escape there. Everyone was killed and they were mostly from my hometown, Satu-Mare. I knew a lot of them. Nothing really changed from this; we were just put in another place to sleep.

People have asked me how we were treated. I once witnessed the hanging of a young Russian. He escaped from the camp and he was the first one ever to escape. They caught him after two weeks and they hanged him in front of everyone. Everybody had to be present. And then another time, there was a father with two young sons. They were from my town. I knew them very well; I don't remember their names. The older boy escaped by hiding in a wagon. Trains used to come in to a working place and he hid in the wagon and that is how he escaped. The Kapos beat the father and the other son very badly; they should tell where the son had escaped. And of course they didn't know. They caught the son who escaped and then they beat all three to death. I saw them being beaten. Here is another example: there were a lot of beatings going on, people died from beatings. I've seen one man from Satu-Mare, he was taken out from the hospital because there was one man who had died that morning and then they were one short. So when they took him out from hospital, he leaned on two men and that's how he walked to the train. And when we arrived to work, he couldn't work. There was a German Sergeant Major, I remember him very well. I can see him before my eyes. He beat the man from Satu-Mare to death and they carried him back dead.

And remember my two close friends that I mentioned? One committed suicide; he hanged himself, and the other one, we slept together, and by the way, we always slept with our clothing on. And I remember he was very handy with a needle, and he got another cap and he sewed it onto my cap so it would cover my ears and keep my ears warm. One day when we went to work, we arrived at the train, and he fell and hurt his knee and he couldn't walk. And so before we went in he gave me his jumper, he told me that he didn't think he would be needing it because we knew that anybody that couldn't work would not come out of there alive. That evening when I returned to camp, they found that other jumper on me. And they sentenced me to get forty lashes. Not the German officers, but the Kapos. It was the head Kapo, from the room where we slept, and there was another Kapo that he told to give me the lashes. That was a Jewish Kapo that gave me the lashes, with a rubber truncheon. He stopped at twenty, because he was told to stop because I didn't cry out. That was a Polish Jew, who had been in camp already for four years. And I never again saw my friend Bernard. He probably died, or they took him to Mauthausen.

I kept working, I had to. The food didn't change. I remember once the food was spilled on the ground when they were carrying it, and we all were fighting to pick up from the ground whatever we could. The food was very bad and the worst part was that there wasn't enough of it. I don't remember how much we got but it couldn't have been more than five hundred to six hundred calories a day. I had a very good stomach. Those who had a bad stomach, they died in the first few weeks. They couldn't eat that food and I was lucky.

I didn't get sick until March. I got a wound on my leg and that wound was full of puss. It got very swollen, and luckily by that time the Russians were very close to Melk and we stopped working. We couldn't go to work anymore. I didn't go to hospital with that wound; I knew that if I did, I probably wouldn't come back alive. There were two German doctors there in Melk. One had a reputation of being a cruel man, and the other one was very good. We called him an angel. And he is the one that had given me the certificate to get inside the mountain.

Lots of people had died from the first week that we had arrived there and then probably hundreds every week. And every day a truck left full of bodies that were taken to Mauthausen where they had a crematorium. And then so many had died that Mauthausen couldn't handle it. And so they built a crematorium at Melk. They replaced the dead ones, always, with new ones.

A German officer, I think he was a Captain, was in charge of Melk. I don't remember ever seeing any higher-ranking German officers coming to Melk.[25]

And we came into contact with civilian Austrians. We saw the Austrians at work. They came in to work and they went home. Nothing was done to hide or conceal the atrocities going on in Melk and with the stench every civilian knew what was going on. There was an Austrian engineer, and his father was in charge. The father had a very bad reputation, but the young man was very gentle and he talked to us, and he encouraged us not to despair, and he was telling us that the Germans are doing very badly and it won't be very long.

So now, in Melk, hearing that the Russians were very close, again we had a lot of hope, as we were the ones that were alive, we believed that we would stay alive. Yes, we had a lot of hope. But then after a few days following stopping the work, they announced that those who are sick could go to a special hospital in Mauthausen. We lined up to go in front of the doctors and got closer and closer to the doctors. Suddenly one of the doctors, a Hungarian Jew, said, "Turn around and run because they are all going to their death!" And we ran back into the camp.

A few days later they took us to another camp called Ebensee, it was a similar camp as Melk; they also built factories inside the mountains. I remember we arrived in the nighttime and we saw the smoke coming from the crematorium and we lined up in a very long queue. There were hundreds of us, if not thousands and we saw them going in and not coming out. Each one of us thought that we were going to our death. But instead they took us to a shower, to be disinfected, and then we were taken to hospital. There were four to a bed, a narrow bed. Two on each side. About half of the people did not have a place to sleep, so in the nighttime we slept under the bed. And in the daytime they put us outside, with the wind and the rain it was very cold. Each day they brought a few dead in from outside. In the nighttime everybody got a blanket. The chap who slept next to me, he pinched a blanket from a Kapo and put that blanket over us. And that Kapo, he went to look for it and he found it on me. That Kapo gave me heartache, and I remember his name. His name was Herschowitz. A few days later when somebody died, he then put me in that bed. And so Herschowitz had beaten me, and then he had saved my life. Because Herschowitz had gotten me into that bed, then I had a good chance to survive, because those that didn't have a bed had only a small chance of surviving since they got thrown outside every morning. There was a special reason for that, so that they should die. They had orders that so many should die.

Do you see this scar on my forehead? I got this from the German Kapo named Hoffman that was in charge. He was from a small town in Czechoslovakia. He was a very bad man. He beat us a lot and he beat me with a cane.

I was just thinking about something in Melk. The chief Kapo was a Gypsy prisoner, and he was very good looking, like a film star. And he was very cruel. No, I don't remember his name but the reason I am suddenly thinking about him, although I didn't see this myself—when I returned to Ebensee; I was told that the Russian prisoners had thrown him alive into the crematorium. And the other Kapos escaped, because if they had not, they probably would have been imprisoned.

Chapter Four

The Krupp Factory was a weapons manufacturer in Altenburg, Thuringia in Eastern Germany, and twenty-five miles south of Dresden near the Czech border. The Altenburg Slave Labor Camps were mostly HASAG operations and sub-camps of Buchenwald.[26] This factory was part of the Krupp German industrialists empire, the largest employer of slave labor in Nazi Germany. Gustov Krupp von Bohlen and his son Alfried negotiated directly with the SS Gestapo for concentration camp inmates. They were in favor of the mass murder of all Jews, Gypsies, and others, but believed that first they should contribute to Germany by supplying a lifetime of work in just months. Hitler accepted the Krupps proposal to use Jewish slave labor. By the end of the war Krupp had used approximately 100,000 slaves, who subsisted in barbaric conditions in over one hundred Krupp factories. Approximately 70,000 slaves died as a result of the savage beatings and torture by the guards for the slightest infraction.[27]

∾

EDITH: Yes, we were slaves in Egypt. Collectively, that is. We always say that we were slaves in Egypt because we never know when we will be again, although 'Never Again' is what we always say now. My people had this history of being enslaved and we built the pyramids. Cruel Pharaohs, and then cruel Nazis along with those German industrialists drooling for profits gained by Jewish slaves.[28] Do you own a Krups Coffeemaker? They have changed the spelling of their name now, but it is that same family.

The Germans hadn't allowed their women to work in factories, at least not until the very end of the war. So here we were. Working on the line, making munitions which we knew were to be used to bomb the American Allies and others who were coming to free us. For twelve or more hours every day, we were slaving on the machines, no breaks and beaten daily for any infraction. Not much food to sustain us. It was awful tasting, lousy, stinking soup with charcoal in it, and one bowl per day, if even that. The big bonus was that we had real toilets that flushed. This was only because the factory wasn't built for Jewish slaves, but for real workers, who would need to relieve themselves in decent facilities. I never told anyone about having real toilets there, because I thought it was too much of a luxury; what would people think?

Those bastards, the German SS guards, we knew that they were the worst of the worst. One day I decided to sabotage the machine that I was working on. Just a little move, to make the bombs crooked, would help the Allies. But I was caught doing this, and I got a beating that may have killed another. Not me though, I was invincible; survival was my destiny. I knew it all along that they couldn't destroy me, at least not physically. I had to stay strong for the others. My sister Hilda needed me, and the other girls needed a leader. I refused to let the SS bastards have the satisfaction of killing me. In prison, I learned a lesson never taught in school or by my parents. Though wisdom was prolific in our home, it was not anticipated being in chains. There seemed no need to learn the art of survival. They plucked my flower but the roots were alive. I nourished it with tender care. Night and day I talked and sang songs until it started sprouting. Leaves with thorns grew with bolts of lightning. Though meek in size, I was strong in spirit, felt no hurt as the striking whip, like a snake curled around it, found its mark.

A Gestapo that we named Big Head also came with us from Auschwitz. We called him that because he had an enormous head and a big square face. He looked like a bulldog. He was completely bald and had huge ears. That day that I had sabotaged the shells, Big Head called me into the office and said to me, "Why did you do this?" I thought to myself, 'Here I am today and I might be dead tomorrow,' so I had to get it out of me', and so I said, "Because I had to." And he said to me, "You know when you get all those shells out of your machine you have to examine every one." The diameter of the machine part was about four inches and on the bottom, if you can imagine, the machine spit out the shells. I had gloves on, so-called gloves out of material that had holes in every finger. The metal slivers and shards all went into my fingers. That was a deadly, treacherous thing to go back with. And I knew that I had to do it, sabotage my machine. We had a Frenchman working there with us who I had asked where these ammunitions that we were working on were going. He told me that they were being used against the Allies. This Frenchman was very educated and he knew everything from before the war. And what did I do with those machines? Well, I had the entire tools: hammer, pliers, wrench, chisel, and all those things. I had to measure how small that I had to cut the metal, even using sharp knives to cut the metal. I was taught how to open all these machines, and close them at the end of the day. The machines were very big, at least a foot taller than I was. The smell of it and the treachery, it was awful. I can even smell it now. So that day, I just didn't make things fit the way that they were supposed to and Big Head the Kapo, the SS Gestapo bastard, he had some belts hanging there on the hanger there that held their coats. He took one of those belts, which was leather and had some kind of a nail on it, and he said, "Why did you do it? Tell me again." And I said, "Because of all the planes that come and bomb Germany, I don't want to be the cause of them dropping out of the sky."

That was the worst beating that I had gotten but there was one thing that I had that they didn't: as we were walking to and from work, I was thinking about Snow White and the Seven Dwarfs. I was remembering that I had painted a picture of Snow White and the Dwarfs for my niece Greta and I had all of the memories and fantasies that I created in my brain. They couldn't take that from me! And also I kept talking to all the girls around me, I had a lot of stories to tell. There were fourteen of us girls that clung together every night. We were so very cold. I don't remember ever having a blanket there.

The Jewish Kapo that we were with in Auschwitz followed us to Krupp. She had a daughter with her, I would say close to thirty years old. The Kapo was a Polish Jew, the same one we called Blokova, which meant Kapo of the Block. She had long hair, which meant she had been there a long time. They slept in the bunk right behind us. Blokova picked Hilda and me a lot for extra duties. She liked us and she knew that we were sisters. We volunteered a lot for extra duty, because it meant more soup. So when she asked who would want to help, we always raised our hands. Mostly we did all the cleaning. Hilda was always a good cleaner back home; she took pride in keeping the floors polished. So after our shift in the munitions factory, we would come back to the barracks and wash the floors and clean.

One time when they asked for volunteers, they only chose me. This time I went to the railroad station to help unload boxes of tomatoes for the SS Gestapos' meals. I had pockets and managed to steal four tomatoes and when I got back I gave them to Hilda. While I was there at the railroad station, there were also boxes filled with hundreds of pairs of shoes. I was able to get a pair of shoes for myself, but I didn't want to think about where those shoes came from.

One day I was in the infirmary at Krupp. A friend of mine had lost a finger in one of the machines; she was bleeding tremendously and the nurse, who was Jewish, pulled up her own skirt and injected the pain shot in her own leg, for herself! That time I was there for what looked like scarlet fever. I had collapsed from overwork and malnutrition. I had fainted at the machine. Do you wonder why they even had an infirmary at Krupp? They needed to keep us alive, to work.

The Gypsies at Krupp were German and we didn't speak to them, even though we spoke German. We stayed away from them because they were very, very mean. They made knives out of their spoons by grinding them on the concrete floor. We were terribly afraid of them because they were extremely violent when they were away from their families. When we knew them back home and they were in a family unit, it was a different story. At Krupp they had a trick, when we were all going down the stairs they would trip one girl and everyone would then fall on top of each other. And then when everyone had gone down, we were supposed to sit on the floor and the Gypsies would start beating their hands on whatever was there, to a rhythm and then started dancing the wild Gypsy dances. They hated us Jews, and called us the Stinking Yudah.

At Krupp, a woman that was in the same bunk that I was in hated me because she was Katzender's cousin and she thought that I had mistreated her cousin. Well, I told her my whole innocent story, that I was fourteen years old when Katzender was looking at me and started following me everywhere. I told her that he wore a ring that had a little latch that opened, and inside, it had my picture in it. I didn't ask him for the bicycle he bought for me in Satu-Mare. To me he was already an old man; he even looked like Spencer Tracy. Then the woman wanted to sleep next to me because I had the reputation of being the best sleeper and a good sleeper. What that meant was that I slept quietly, I didn't move around and I wasn't a quarreling type. Yes, people had their reputations. And whatever their reputation was, it stuck with the people.

I want to talk about the last day at Krupp.[29] First, I have to tell you that at the factory there was an old German guard who looked like he was in the war but he didn't really want to be there. Even in Auschwitz, there were sometimes one German or one Polish doctor that might have some mercy on you and do some small thing that might save your life. So off and on this old German would tell me certain things, like just before we were told to line up and start going, walking, I asked him "What do you think is going on here?" And he told me, "The Americans are thirty kilometers away from us and we have to evacuate." I don't know exactly how many of the guards were around us, by us. They were the most horrible SS guards that were around the factory that took us. We started walking in a line. They were watching the way we were walking, and off and on hitting us girls back and forth, in order to get us to keep going.

The one thing I do remember distinctly: we had stopped in front of this house on the street where we were walking and all of a sudden I saw this old German woman, she grabbed her face and I could hear her talking to a person next to her and she said, "Oh my God what's going on there?" And then she ran into her house and came out and she had something in her hand and she handed it to me. I looked at it; it was a pair of socks that she gave me. I don't believe that I ever told anyone this part of the story. And, I was so shocked and bewildered that I didn't know if I should cry or laugh from joy having those nice socks in my hand. I sat on the sidewalk and I put them on because by that time I was completely without shoes, I was barefooted. And there is something related to this story about the socks that I didn't want to tell before because it sounded so ridiculous. It's a funny thing that every time I go to buy something I always buy two of something because I always have that fear that I'll lose what I bought and won't have it anymore.

So, we didn't have much clothing. The only thing we had was one garment; maybe a long dress or whatever was left over from the other dead people that they left behind. Whatever we could grab we put it on us but we were very cold. So we kept marching. Off and on the girls would stop and some died next to me or they got hurt. I tried to help somebody to keep on walking and the SS, whoever was following me, hit me on my back. And so we had to keep on walking the way we were. Anyway, it was tragic, it was desperate. We were starving and as we were walking, it was farmland and it was forests.

We walked five days, by day and by night.[30] We were actually walking on the battlefield, with bombs bursting all over. And the only break we got for a few minutes in all the hours was when the Allies and the bombs were getting very close so we had to go under trees. That was the only chance that we had to sit down or go to the bathroom, which we had to do on the ground. Apparently the Americans were coming closer. I could hear the planes above and when it was light enough I could see that they were silver, they were flying pretty low. And so we knew they were American planes. We were cold, very cold. In Europe, April is very cold. It doesn't start warming up until May. The most horrible thing that I can think of, I don't want to say. I think everything was pretty horrible.

After the fifth night we came to a barn. And right before we approached the area where the barn was, we saw mounds of dirt, with what looked like potatoes or something like that sticking out of the dirt. But then we saw what it was. It was turnips! We started grabbing the turnips and digging the dirt with our fingers and eating the turnips along with the dirt. We didn't care, we were so hungry, and we swallowed the dirt. The Germans, those SS Gestapo bastards, they beat us up so bad we had to drop the turnips and start running from them and by this time came near a farmhouse. And you know what? To this day I hate to eat turnips, I can't even put them in chicken soup. Do you believe it? Turnips can trigger bad memories.

So we got near this farmhouse and they made us go into the barn and they closed us in. We heard some commotion outside. They started talking, in German, that they have to light the fire and leave the girls locked in the barn. Since I understand German, I knew what they were plotting. They intended to set the barn on fire with us inside. It must have been very close to twelve o'clock noon because suddenly the church bells started ringing. And then everything was so silent. I told the girls to stay put, while I peeked out to see what was going on there. I opened up the gate. That door was easy to open and I ran out. I couldn't see anybody. All the Germans were gone. I ran back to the girls, altogether there were about seventy of us. And then I went back out on the road by myself, it seemed that the Germans ran away somewhere. Suddenly I saw the Jeeps. At this point I wasn't sure yet if they were Americans. After that, one soldier came close to me, and I could see by the green uniforms that they were wearing that they were American soldiers. There was a general with them, he had five stars on his shirt, and I understood when he asked the soldiers, in English, "Who is this girl and what is she doing here?" The other girls were still in the barn; I was the only girl outside because I hadn't yet told the girls that it was O.K. to come out. One of the soldiers said to the general, "This girl speaks English, General." The General turned to me and he said, "Were you in prison?" And so I told him where we had come from and he said, "Is this what they did to you, those son of a bitches?" I can't forget that! That was one of General Patton's divisions, the 4th Armored Division. There was a whole battalion of American GIs with a lot of tanks and Jeeps.

I went inside the barn and told the girls it was O.K. to come out now. This place was called Meerane, Silesia in Germany. And now the story gets very interesting. For six days right after April 13th there was a villa that we stayed in. The American soldiers had found us a gorgeous house where six of us girls stayed, and the war wasn't over yet. The Germans were five kilometers from us and you could hear the bombs bursting.

We somehow managed to stay together throughout. I was always hopeful. I had to be, for all the girls around me. They looked to me for that, to keep going. And so we found ourselves here at this villa, right after liberation, with the American GIs standing guard over us, day and night, to protect all of us girls.

And then after that, we went into the farmhouse. You see, after the six days at the villa, the Captain of the whole team came in and told us that we were going back to where the barn was, where we were first found. He gave the farmers, the owners of the place, orders to take care of us girls and to feed us and give us a bath every day. They had a daughter who was our age, and she had to help take care of us, too. In this farmhouse, and it was just a plain farmhouse, not a villa, the six of us girls were allotted to stay here.

The rest of the girls were put in similar types of situations. And we stayed here for about four weeks. The farmers, the husband and wife were scared to death, I could tell. But they never talked, they were just very serious and they were just jumping if we told them anything. We didn't have any beds but they took the whole floor of a room and put mattresses down enough to cover for six girls. And they had a toilet inside, but for baths there was a big tub in the kitchen where they had to prepare warm water for us every day, and we bathed in that. The food was absolutely wonderful, they really fattened us up. And we were just so happy not to be starved. They cooked all the good German food. We had all we could want to eat. We started to look better; our hair was growing back. And then soon after, we started to notice the American GIs because they started to come around.

And suddenly, there was this one American GI, his name was Joe Fletcher. He was from Oregon. There is a photograph of some GIs dancing, and Joe Fletcher is there in it; you can see how handsome he was! And it was sort of a 'get to know somebody' and suddenly there were feelings for each other. I kissed him, he was nice. His kindness was overwhelming. He liked me so much. I only knew him a couple of days and he had to go back to the war, and well, the war was still on. He had given me a diamond ring, and I had just accepted it! You see, the word had gotten around with the American GIs that there were girls living at the farmhouse and Joe had come around.

So, around Meerane there were a lot of GIs running around and they were all very nice to us, and trying to impress us. Anyway, the one that I really liked, in fact I was crazy about him; his name was Lee Wasserman, he was gorgeous! He gave me a photo of himself, and he wrote on the back, 'To a lovely sweet tomato.' And he had a revolver in his pocket and it was made out of white mother of pearl. I kissed him, too. He was marvelous. He taught me the first American songs. He brought a little gramophone when he came over; you know where you put the record on. But I think Lee became very sad, because he asked me whether I believed in God and I said to him, "How can I?" And he said, "You shouldn't talk like that." And I said to him, "No kidding, you know it was one year ago already that I lost my whole family." And after that, I guess he didn't want to come back because I looked so sad. He vanished, he went back. I suppose it sounds like there was a lot of knocking on my door, over there in Meerane, at the farmhouse. I did have some admirers but I liked Lee the best. Too bad that I never heard from him again.

The reason I had so many boyfriends coming around is because they heard that there were girls that were in the concentration camp, and that they lived in the farmhouse. All these guys were Jewish except for Joe Fletcher, and so they came to see the Jewish girls.

The American soldiers did some really cute things for us. They used to go outside at night and kill the chickens. They thought they were making us feel good but we weren't feeling good from it! And there was a small town near us and we would go there by bicycle to visit and the bicycles were provided to us from the German locals. The American GIs watched over us girls. These boys were so American, and so nice.

I want to mention the topic of revenge here. I am referring to the so-called Jewish Revenge.[31] When we were at the farmhouse, getting those bicycles that we used to ride into town was the only revenge that we got. During this period of about fourteen days when we first were liberated, we knew there was no organized law. The Captain that was in charge of us girls was very angry about what he saw, about what had happened to us. It seemed like he needed to say something for his own self-satisfaction. He said,

"Don't worry about anything, God will help you." and I thought again, "What God?" It was obvious at the time of liberation that there was no law. But I did not want any revenge. There was enough of war and of killings. We just wanted to live in peace. So we just took the bicycles, which was good enough.

I have to tell you something very important here. After a few weeks we saw Russian soldiers in the town, so we went to ask around to find out what's going on. We were told that when the Americans occupied a place, a city or an area, they gave it over to the Russians, because the Russians were taking over all the areas that the Americans captured. I'm not going to tell you why they did that. I'm not mixing in politics here. So, when the American GIs told us that the Russians would be coming in they didn't say what we should expect from the Russians. Well, they didn't have to tell me, because I had heard plenty of stories about the Russians back home in Hungary, where I came from. There was gossip going around Meerane, a lot of gossip. I didn't think that the Russians were any worse than any other soldier in the war. But still, we had to get out of there because we were scared and I was only guessing as to what the Russian soldiers were really like.

And then there was the Major: Doctor Max Goodman. This American, Major Max Goodman, arranged for us girls to be transported to Munich by freight train. We were to first go to Bamberg, and then on to Munich. It was an overnight trip.

We were going with boxes of sugar, and the American GIs would sleep in another freight car. This was a freight car with sliding doors. You may be wondering if it reminded me of the deportation train to Auschwitz; but it didn't! I felt just fine about getting onto a freight train this time! Because just the idea that the soldiers were American; you mention Americans, and all bad things get erased. Right away we felt good. We felt secure. We slept right on top of the boxes of sugar and the GIs gave us blankets. And that first night, they stopped the train for a while and we all got outside and they built a campfire. One of the soldiers had a guitar. They started singing and they taught us a song or two and we sang along with them. We were having a wonderful time. My sister Hilda and I were the only girls that spoke English, so we translated to Hungarian when we had to. And I remember exactly what the songs were ...La la-la-la-la! San Antonio... and another one was ...Sweet and lovely, sweet as the roses in May and she loved me...la la-la la, la-la-la-la...

After a while we got back on the train and went to the Bamberg Station and spent the night there. We slept in the office, where the Bamberg station manager, who was a U. S. Captain, had set up cots for us girls to sleep on. He took good care of us. As I think back, I remember getting ready for bed that night. I looked at the cot that I would sleep on and I wasn't thinking of the Americans as strangers or soldiers in war. I just embraced it all with gratitude, all that they gave us. I was remembering all the miles that I left behind; the distance kept growing as we left the past behind. Every mile grew longer and longer and at that moment the pain continued to diminish. In the morning we ate oranges.

And we arrived at the train station in the city of Munich. We felt good, we had some decent clothing. I remember that I was wearing short pants and a man's shirt with the sleeves rolled up. The weather had started warming up, it was almost June. Although

I saw thousands of refugees in the streets, I was very calm at this point because we knew we had a place to go. Everything was so well organized, planned out by Major Max Goodman.

MENDI: I think it was on the 7th of May 1945, after being in Ebensee for a few days that the Americans arrived. They took me to a place called Bad Auzay and they put me into a hospital; this time it was real hospital. I remember eating day and night. They weighed me in that hospital and I was thirty-five kilograms.[32] I had a very, very long beard. I was dark in color from lack of vitamins and I had that terrible wound. They asked my age and when I told them that I was twenty-nine, they wouldn't believe it. They thought I was at least forty. But I recovered quite quickly. They treated my leg and my lung was a little bit affected, but apparently I recovered from that too.

The food was good. I had two people with me in my room. One was from Satu-Mare and could have been in his forties; I remember he had one finger missing from his hand. He died after a week or so. There was a young man too, and one day he got mad and ran out into the woods. I was there for about three weeks.

And then they took me back to Ebensee. We were there for a week or so. And then they announced that those who wanted to register to go to Palestine should sign up. And we also had the choice to go home. I chose to go back home because I was hoping that my two sisters, Hilda and Edith, had possibly a chance, being young, to survive. I wanted to see if they were back in Satu-Mare.

I got back by taking different trains. I got to Budapest and the Jewish organization was waiting there to meet us and gave most of us clothing and fed us well and then put us on another train to go home.

When I got back to Satu-Mare, I walked home. It wasn't far from the train station downtown, only about one half kilometer to our home, which was at 21 Attila Street. Pictures of the parents were there and furniture and all of my father's books. He had a lot of books, a big library. And when I saw the pictures of my parents I got sick. So, there were other people there with me and they took me to the hospital. There was a Jewish hospital on the street where our house was. I didn't take anything with me from the house. Of course I am very, very sorry about that. There was one book that was in the family for about one hundred fifty years and it had the family tree in it. My father had a set of bibles, the five books, and so did my grandfather. I didn't take anything. But later I heard that an uncle of mine, who lived in Arad, came and got some of the books.

After a few days an old family friend arrived. It was Katzender Tule, and he had survived Auschwitz. He was in love with my sister Edith. I was in hospital for a few weeks, and then Katzender took me to his place. I was still sick with my leg. It took quite a few months till I could walk well.

EDITH: After liberation when Mendi went back to Satu-Mare, Katzender told him that I was alive. I wondered how Katzender found out that Hilda and

I had survived? Maybe my bunkmate from Krupp, Katzender's cousin, told him.

MENDI: While I was in Satu-Mare, I had gone to the Red Cross. I was looking for my sister Helen and brother-in-law Jules who lived in Sydney, Australia. And they told me that they would try to find them for me.

And then Mordecai Stauber, a cousin of mine, arrived. He wanted me to go and live with him. I was there with him till, I think December, and he told me that there was a transport going to Palestine. There was a Jewish organization that was arranging it for those that wanted to, would be able to go. I chose to go, but then Katzender found out that Edith and Hilda were alive, and living in Munich. He had their address; I can still remember that it was Ganghofer Strasse in Munich. So my cousin Maty, that's what we called him, arranged for me to go with that Palestine transport as far as Munich. It took a few weeks. We went as far as Budapest and there they arranged for us to stay with a Jewish family until there would be another train coming bound for Munich. We took different trains, sometimes they turned us back and then we went with another train until we got to Munich.

Chapter Five

The American Jewish Joint Distribution Committee, a voluntary Jewish organization, had been founded in 1914. Between 1933 and 1938 JDC helped 250,000 German Jews and 125,000 Austrian Jews run from Europe. After 1940, thousands more Jews fled the Nazis with JDC's help. After Pearl Harbor, the JDC worked through neutral embassies and the International Red Cross to help Jews in occupied Europe and Shanghai. After World War II ended, the JDC organized a massive relief effort and became the main Jewish agency supporting survivors throughout Europe. They provided material support, helped in emigration, and helped reestablish Jewish life. The Red Cross played an important role in aiding Holocaust survivors. The Red Cross Holocaust and War Victims Tracing Center is a national clearinghouse for persons seeking the fates of loved ones missing since the Holocaust and its aftermath, and still exists.

༄

EDITH: I am estimating that I arrived in Munich on June 1st, 1945, give or take a day. Or maybe it was even a week before that, I am not really sure. I arrived in a boxcar, with the six of us Jewish girls sitting on the boxes of sugar, guarded by American GIs. I remember that first day, when I arrived in Munich, the exact moment that I got off of that train. And how can I ever forget that day? That was such a day! Yes, I had a wonderful, wonderful day. In the midst of all the pandemonium on the streets of Munich, with thousands of refugees converging on the city, the sun was shining right on me! It was with the help of Major Dr. Max Goodman who arranged for us to meet a couple of people from the Jewish Committee, the JDC, who were involved with procuring apartments or locations where we could stay. They met us at the train station and drove us over to 56 Ganghofer Strasse where we were delegated to this apartment place. My sister and I were given a gorgeous apartment.

When I had stepped off of that train that day, I could not help thinking that for all that the Germans had done to us, fate had spit the Jews right back on them, on that glorious day when the Jews were free and we arrived in Munich.

My first impression of the new apartment in Munich was so positive. It looked like any modern apartment. And of course it was fabulous for us because this was the first time since we were captured by the Germans and put in camps, for us to live in a gorgeous apartment, our own place. Amazing! It was completely furnished; everything was there: linens, dishes, and furniture. Whoever lived there before, the Germans, they ran! And they left everything behind. So it came wonderfully handy for us. One room, a bedroom, had a big heater built into the wall. It was a real fireplace. There was a building manager and he kept us supplied with the heating materials, black coal. For a while all of us six girls lived there. Then I made some of them move into another one of the apartments in the same building. My sister Hilda and our girlfriend Miki stayed with me.

HILDA: After liberation, Edith and I lived in great comfort in Meerane for some weeks. And then we went to Munich and we were provided a luxury apartment in a building that was requisitioned from Germans. A doctor who was imprisoned by the Americans, I think. The wife was a Danish nurse, who returned back to her home. Of course, you can imagine how that nurse felt? Nevertheless she stayed in one room in the apartment. We had the bath. That was terrific. It was good to be alive and free!

EDITH: We were on the first floor, but one up. We had a beautiful bathroom. The kitchen was nice and complete with pots and pans and a refrigerator. There was even a patio, but we didn't actually have the time to use it much because we were too busy trying to get jobs. But of course looking for work ended right away because since Hilda and I were fluent in English, the job offers came very fast. It was not more than a couple of days after getting settled into the apartment that the leaders of the American USO offered us jobs at one of their camps.[33] We accepted, and they drove us into the mountains in a Jeep. We were supposed to be the managers of the new place they were opening up to entertain the American soldiers.

It was a long drive; it took about five hours to get there. And that night we slept in a hotel, and it was the first time since we were liberated that I was in a hotel. I was so shocked because there was a clock, and the ticking kept me awake the whole night. I wasn't used to hearing things like that, and also I was hearing little birds chirping in the trees. Anyway, I didn't like it there because Hilda and I were the only girls and there were too many guys there. It was all too shocking for us. I liked the traffic, the noise of the city of Munich and already I felt homesick. I didn't want to be in the mountains. I'm not sure where we were; it might have been near Garmisch-Parten. It was some type of former German building that had been an entertainment center, and the Americans had taken it over.

While we were there we were singing songs for the soldiers, all kinds of songs like the ones we had learned from the GIs we had met so far. And we served them coffee and the delicious donuts that they cooked right there. There was a dance floor, but there was no one for the GIs to dance with, except Hilda and me! After a few days we went to the two soldiers that had driven us up there and explained to them that we wanted to go back to Munich, that we were lonely and needed to be with the people that we were with before. They understood and drove us back to Munich.

A few days after returning from that adventure we started working at Radio Munich. Hilda and I got the jobs with the Armed Forces Network through some friends.[34] It was secretarial work, writing up the news on paper, mostly in English and some in German. All the music was strictly American and I loved that they played all American music. They wanted me to write up my story to be read on the airwaves. It was a condition for getting hired.

While I was working at Radio Munich, I got a letter from Joe Fletcher, the GI from Meerane. He said that he had heard on the radio that I was working there. He said, "How come you didn't write to me, and just left me like that?" I thought he had left me, really, so I was very surprised. But then when I heard him identify himself like that six weeks later, I was so scared that I had gotten engaged to him. I never wanted to see him again! Only because he wasn't Jewish. He told me to keep the diamond ring, and later, I gave it to my niece in Amsterdam.

HILDA: We worked in the Radio Station with the Americans and Germans together. Edith was always very intelligent. She learned faster than I did. They taught us office work to do, in order to help us. It was terrific because the Americans wanted to help us in every way.

EDITH: I loved working at Radio Munich. I made wonderful friends there. One of the disc jockeys, Mr. Caplan, was one of my best friends. Hilda and I were the only Hungarians working there. My co-workers were all American and all men. There was just one other woman working there; Maria, and she was German. She became my friend, she was very nice. And after awhile she and my brother Mendi became lovers.

HILDA: Once, Edith and I were away visiting friends in another city for a few days. Returning home we found our brother Mendi and a cousin in our home, it was a big surprise, as we thought Auschwitz murdered him and he was alive. Just was our joy!

MENDI: We arrived in Munich in the night, with about a half a dozen people that had come with me. When we got to 56 Ganghofer Strasse, I rang the bell several times before a woman answered. She looked very frightened, and we asked to see Edith and Hilda Festinger. She told us that they were away for the evening and they would be returning in the morning. It was this woman's flat, which was requisitioned from the American Army. She was allowed one room, and she had to turn the other rooms over to my sisters and the other Jewish girls.

The next morning when my sisters arrived, they saw all those people sleeping on the floor. At first they got a fright until they saw me and then they got the surprise of their lives because they thought that I was taken, in Auschwitz, to the left, and they were sure that I had died. And there I was! You can imagine their happiness.

EDITH: My brother Mendi, who we thought had been murdered with our parents in Auschwitz suddenly showed up in Munich! We had a wonderful reunion! Have you ever thought someone that you loved was dead and then they show up? It was incredible!

MENDI: Shortly after I arrived in Munich, in fact just a few days later, I found out that the Red Cross had found Helen and Jules de Leeuw in Sydney, and gave them the news that I had survived. A permit arrived for me; it was my Australian Landing Permit that had been issued. Edith and Hilda had been in touch with them in Sydney, but they had written to them that I had died. I stayed in Munich with my sisters for about six months.

EDITH: When you had one American friend or a soldier, the jobs and all the other stuff followed. We didn't even need money, not that the German money was worth anything anyway. But we didn't have to spend anything because everywhere that we went, somebody paid for us.

My cousin Janka Festinger worked in a donut factory and so we had all the donuts we could possibly eat. Not the kind that you see today, but the original old fashioned ones. They were made from heavy dough that was like cake, and yellowish in color. And when you bit into these donuts, they crumbled. There was white powdered sugar sprinkled on the outside. Messy but delicious!

There wasn't any food anywhere, but for us, the GIs stocked the food very fast in our apartment. They brought us everything and it was fun! During this time we didn't think about where our meals would be coming from. Isn't that funny? After starving like we did, suddenly food wasn't important.

One thing I do remember is that my brother-in-law that was in Sydney, Jules de Leeuw, sent us many, many boxes of food from Australia. And he had a friend in New York that worked for a tuna fish company who sent us boxes of tuna. That was new to me. I thought it was chicken. And we ate that day and night. That is probably why I am not crazy about eating tuna now.

People brought their own food into restaurants and pubs. And every day we took our lunch and we went out into a place called the Lowenbrau Keller.[35] And you went down stairs to get in, and you could almost say it was under the house. This was one of the places that Hitler had given speeches at. And after Hitler disappeared, the Jewish people, like me, took it over completely. And that is where we all met and we made a club out of it. I loved to go there and drink American Coca-Cola.

NATE: I was in the U.S. Army in Nuremberg at the end of the war. My company was put on laundry detail. We took washing trucks to American camps. These trucks had washing machines mounted right on the truck, with their own motors and generators.

Then I got assigned to Munich, Germany for the rest of 1945 through Spring of 1946. They had called twelve of us men and a sergeant to go to Munich to handle all the cold food storage for the American Army in Europe. It was called the Munich Cool House. I did shipping and receiving and lived on the army base. My occupational specialty was Supply Clerk. The first floor of the Cool House had a giant kitchen, a dining room lounge, and living room. The second floor had four to five rooms.

There were three German cooks for twelve American soldiers. The cooks made ice sculptures for us twelve U.S. soldiers and baked cakes for us. The three cooks were terrific! Polish soldiers guarded the Cool House. You had to have permits to get in. The MPs would have to pick up these Polish guys because they were continuously out after curfew and carrying guns. Then we had to bail these guys out, so we gave extra food to the MPs. And officers were trading whiskey and cigarettes for food.

HILDA: On one occasion Edith and I were traveling on a tram in Munich and suddenly the bus conductor asked us to get up from our seats to make room for the wounded German soldiers. We refused him. We said, "Let the young Germans get up from their seats, we were in Auschwitz long enough." Next thing, Edith stepped off from the moving tram and as I started to follow her, the conductor grabbed me by my throat and all the Germans on the bus were shouting "Out with the Jews!" I was standing in the middle of the tram in order to stop the tram, which was standard. It stopped. A young German boy went with Edith and me to the American Military Police to be a witness. The American Police were very nice, flirting with two young girls. At the end they told us to go to the Civilian German Police Station, where we didn't wish to go. Just some months after liberation, such a terrible experience shouldn't have happened then, traveling in town. We just let it go.

EDITH: You are probably wondering what I had to wear in those days. Well, I had all the clothes that I could use because my girlfriend, our roommate Miki, was a dressmaker. She didn't have a job because she didn't speak German or English. She only spoke Hungarian and Romanian. She was the one that made us clothes out of everything that the GIs brought us, including parachutes! In the photograph on my French Visa, I am wearing a beautiful white blouse that Miki made out of a parachute.

During this time there was a lot of social activity going on because most of the other people that we met needed to find a place to live, and they came to me, as I was the one who was able to tell them how to get it. So, if friends came in from another place, like people from Romania looking for survivors, friends, or family, they came to me to find out the details as to how to approach such matters. And so I let them sleep in our apartment, and at times you could see as many as ten to fifteen people sleeping on the floor, even more.

My cousin Gizi Festinger's husband was in Munich and we met there. In fact, he was in the crowd that I ran around with. His name was Stauber; there were a lot of Staubers around. Gizi and her baby had perished but her husband had somehow survived.

One day Major Max Goodman came back onto the scene. Max tried to see me, during the time I was working at Radio Munich. He showed up at my apartment unannounced. I didn't know that he was in Munich. I was busy at that time. He found me kissing another soldier. He was upset. He slammed the door and stormed out. He left and never saw me again. And you know what? I couldn't have cared less. I suppose that sounds cold hearted after everything that Max did for me, in setting me up with everything and helping me to get settled.

But I would like to tell you the truth about Max. Something had happened with him that I have kept secret all these years. For the truth, we have to go back to Meerane, after we were liberated. I never told anyone about this because I think I was just pretending it didn't happen. One day in Meerane, not too long after we were settled in the farmhouse, Max came to see me. I don't exactly remember the first time that I had seen Max, or met him, as we were so disoriented at first. But after a few weeks, he came again to the farmhouse. He just showed up, and wanted to give me the photo of himself.

Then, he came again another time. This one time, I think it was the third time that I had seen him, I was alone in the farmhouse and he suddenly violently grabbed me and kissed me. Can you imagine how young I was then? How inexperienced? How abnormal my teenage years were? Like what teenagers usually experience, I had not even gone out on many dates or even kissed boys much at all before this. I think Max was older. I mean, I realized that he was very much older than me. I was a kid, really. I looked like a woman but emotionally, with boys, well, you can imagine. At that time in Meerane, I was not hungry any more, but still very thin, after just two weeks. After the kiss, and it was a real rough kiss, he suddenly went crazy and I thought he was trying to rape me. I was so shocked. He was so forceful; he was wild! He was all over me, trying to touch me. I never had that experience before, I never! You are probably wondering how I got rid of him? He saw that I was serious. I got very nasty. He could see that I was ready to begin screaming. I was fighting him too much. He finally got disgusted with himself and got off of me. During the episode it was like time stood still. It was awful. I cried my eyes out afterwards. After, he vanished. I didn't see him again until he showed up at my apartment in Munich. I thought Max Goodman was my hero. And I remember that I wondered how he knew where I was living. But then I remembered that he had arranged for us to get the apartment and maybe he felt guilty for doing what he did. I was able to get through the war without being molested by Nazis and then this happened with Max Goodman. But at least he stopped before going through with what he had on his mind. And I never told anyone about this. I don't even think I told my sister Hilda. I was very, very disappointed in Max. I thought he was a true hero. I let everyone think that he was.

Greta Meyer, 13 (Edith's niece) murdered at Auschwitz, June 2, 1944

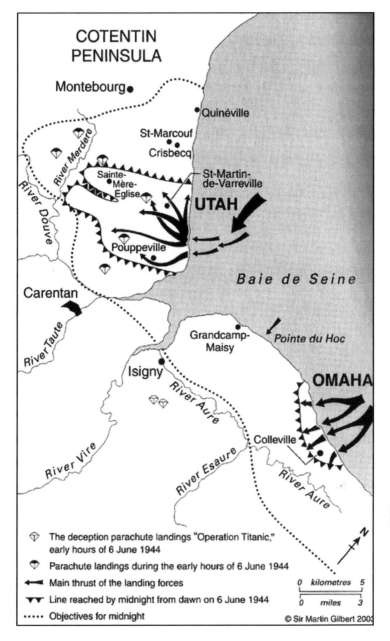

The Utah and Omaha Beach Landings, 6 June 1944
©Martin Gilbert, 2008
THE ROUTLEDGE ATLAS OF THE SECOND WORLD WAR
By Martin Gilbert ISBN 041539709X published by Routledge

Nate Litvin (left) Utah Beach, after
D-Day, June 1944

Krupp Factory, Altenburg, Germany,
April 1945, Photo by Jack Clark

Farmhouse where the liberated girls recovered, Meerane, Silesia, end of April through end of May 1945

GIs in Meerane, Silesia, Joe Fletcher (far right), May 1945

Freight train to Munich, via Bamberg, May 1945

Edith Festinger with GI, en route to Munich via Bamburg, May 1945

Major Max Goodman, U.S. Army 1945

Nate Litvin (middle), Germany 1945

Hilda and Edith Festinger, with GI at the USO job, June 1945

Edith Festinger and John Lury at the Munich apartment, June 1945

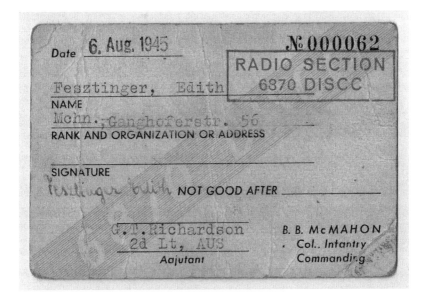

Edith Festinger's Radio Munich ID card, issued August 5, 1945

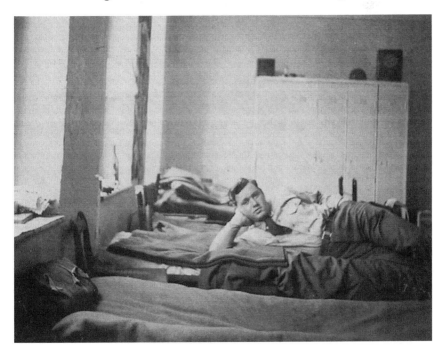

Nate Litvin at the U.S. Army Base Barracks, Munich 1945

Edith Festinger and Nate Litvin, Munich 1946

Nate Litvin (left) at his desk at Cool House, Munich 1945

Survivors, and Those Who Returned, 1945
©Martin Gilbert, 2008
THE ROUTLEDGE ATLAS OF THE HOLOCAUST
3rd Edn by Martin Gilbert ISBN 0415281458 HB
& 0415281466 PB published by Routledge 2002

Part 3

Chapter Six

Journal Entry

3 September 1945
Edith Festinger
56 Ganghofer Str.
Munich, Germany

The past still lingers in my soul. Maybe that is the reason I can not laugh like others do. Now that my stomach is full and I feel no thirst, memories linger and do not let me be. I feel no hate for the enemy that destroyed my family. Harboring such feeling is destructful. Dear Lord, Make my father's wish come true; send a nice Jewish man my way. Let him be the one I marry with all the aching love stored too long inside me and if there is a Heaven let my parents give me their blessing. Make my tears subside. Mama, why did you bring me into this world? Was it inscribed in fate that I am to be separated from my family? Was I meant to live alone? Is this why you freed me, God? Will my destiny be to wander on this earth? Please grant me this wish that I'll find the home that I need so much. O dear God, if ever I marry, I'll be good and loyal to him.

∽

NATE: Edith was so beautiful; all the American soldiers were chasing her around. There was this one I can't forget. His name was Max Goodman. Max had a sweet eye on Edith. He was an American Major running transportation of goods and soldiers. He had gotten acquainted with the Festinger sisters and the other Hungarian girls in Meerane, Silesia. That was where the girls were recovering after their liberation. He was the one who told them that the Russians were coming to take over the area of Meerane. In the middle of the night he put them on a train, in a boxcar filled with sugar, bound for Munich. When the boxcar opened up, six girls appeared!

The war was over and I wanted to meet some Jewish girls. The Lowenbrau Keller, where Hitler used to make famous speeches became a Jewish hangout. I went there with Herschowitz, a Jewish Hungarian friend of mine.[36] He said he would take me to meet some English speaking Jewish girls. My friend told me that Edith and Hilda were two sisters who were really very beautiful Jewish girls that went to the Lowenbrau Keller for lunches. Although I went there two or three times, I didn't see them. I drank beer. I said to my friend, "Where the hell are these girls?" So he took me to their apartment. Both girls worked for Radio Munich and had a nice apartment. When we got there the girls were not there. I went back again another time and then met Mendi Festinger, the girls' brother, and the sisters, Edith and Hilda Festinger. I started dating Edith.

HILDA: We met Nate Litvin on an occasion. He was asking to look for people like us: Edith and me, also Mendi, and our cousin Maty Stauber. He visited us with the offer that he would like to provide us with anything that he could help with.

When we met Nate, Edith had a friendship with a doctor, who was a Captain. His name was John

Lury, and John was crazy about my sister. She felt that way about John also. For quite a long time they were friends.

EDITH: Before I begin to talk about Nate, I have to mention my boyfriend, the main one, who I was seriously dating before I met Nate. His name was Dr. John Lury. He was a captain, a very elegant and aristocratic, somewhat bashful, almost withdrawn man around other people. But with me he laughed all the time. He took me to The Sea House many times. That was an officers' nightclub, where the Captains were dating their girlfriends. There was an orchestra there and we would be dancing and drinking rum and Coca-Cola.

We were very close and I admit that I was in love with John. He was very nice. I remember making stuffed cabbage for him once. It was going to be like his mother made but I didn't put any tomato sauce in it because there wasn't any. And all he said was that his mother made it different. And one day John had brought me a gorgeous harmonica; he knew that I used to play harmonica back home in Hungary. John just absolutely loved that I could play it and wanted me to play for him every time he came over. And I did.

But one time John showed me a picture of a girl; it might have been his girlfriend back home in the States. And so I thought the girl was the one he had back home. Maybe he was already engaged.

One evening after that, John sent his footman over to my apartment with real firewood for the fireplace. And the footman said to me, "My Captain said to tell

Edith, 'I can't come over tonight, I am busy'." And then this footman said, "I brought something for you, too, it's in the Jeep. I'll be right back." And he came back in with a little cooking plate and hot dogs. And he asked me if we could have a picnic. We sat right there on the floor and cooked hot dogs. And then I kissed him. We had a good time. I don't know if he told his Captain, the doctor, about this.

Physically, I was not available to John. He went back to the States knowing that this girl didn't give him anything. By the way, I never slept with any of them. Just kissing. No touching. Back in Hungary, we were brought up that if a girl sleeps with a guy you are a whore. And then no one is ever going to marry you. And so with that on my mind, I was scared to death of that sex life that people carry on with.

And there were some others, some I liked and some that I didn't like so much. There was Abe Green, a GI from New York. He was madly in love with me.[37] He even had his sister, back in the U.S.A. send a box of shoes over for me. I am sorry to say that I broke his heart. One night he cried and begged me to choose him over Nate. And he made me feel so guilty for not choosing him. He acted like he was going to have a nervous breakdown. Actually, I think I met Abe when he was dating one of my friends from Feldafing, the Displaced Persons Camp.[38] That's how he knew me. I wasn't exactly dating Abe. We went for a walk once. I don't remember going out to a club or anything like that with him. He was terribly emotional the whole time and it made me feel weird. I didn't promise him anything. But he got so attached to me. I have to admit that I saw him a few times, and yes, I kissed him a few times, but it wasn't anything specific. I wasn't deeply entangled with him.

I had met Nate sometime around September 1945. I was still working at Radio Munich. After I had been dating Nate for a while he disappeared on me for six weeks. He went to England and during that time that he was gone, I did not hear from him. He did not call or write. I was very angry. I had no idea where he was. Later, he just let it slip out that he had been in England. He had been to England before, in 1943.

Nate also admitted to me that there was a woman that he knew there, in England. She had a child or two. I found a photo from that time. In the photo Nate, another GI, and a woman with blonde hair, are all smiling and there is a small child in a carriage. There are no notes on the back of the photo, but it looks like England. I think that Nate may have sired a child with that woman. The child looks a bit like Nate. This was very, very upsetting to me! The other GI was a friend of Nate's from Puerto Rico. I always wondered if there was a child left behind. I am very jealous when I think of this and I will always wonder if Nate cheated on me.

Never mind that I had another boyfriend! I was dating, yes, but I was dating Nate steady for a couple of months and it was getting serious. Everybody knew that. He did not even say goodbye to me. He just disappeared and I was disappointed, but not for long. I went on with my life. And there were many friends around. We were a tight knit community of survivors. There was a lot going on at that time. Some of the American GIs were dating some girls from Feldafing. I visited Feldafing only once, because to me, it was just another prison. I did go out on some dates at that time. But it was known around that I was Nate's girl, except he had left, so I was unsure.

Then Nate returned from England. Suddenly, there he was. He just knocked on the door, just showed up. I had asked him, "Where were you?" He said he had furlough. I don't even remember him explaining. Really, I think that was his way of getting back at me, for dating the Captain. Yes, that must have been it. Nate didn't show emotions. John Lury was right there and under his nose. He watched us going out and coming back. Yes, I think that Nate went away to get back at me for dating the doctor.

I didn't actually question Nate anymore because his behavior told me that he liked me a lot and he was back where he was supposed to be. We simply started the relationship again; we just picked up from where we were. I just forgot it. I let it go. But the doctor was around, yes. John was still around.

I worked at Radio Munich for about four months. But then the war with Japan had ended.[39] I remember that at that time I was overjoyed because up until then, I was sick with worry for my family that had been in the East Indies. They had been caught up in the war with Japan over there and they were unaccounted for. I knew now that there was hope to find them. I just wanted some time off of work, to try to locate them. It was sometime in September of 1945 that we quit Radio Munich.

KURT: Even though the war with Japan ended, it took me three months to find my family. Sometime around November 1945, with the help of the Red Cross, I found Piri, my mother, sister, and the children, five hundred miles away from Jakarta. Then they came to Jakarta.

We were given the choice to either go to Holland or Australia. We decided on Holland and the next day got ready to go on a boat to Singapore. The trip to Singapore was just one night. But when we got to Singapore, we found that the ship had already left for Holland! We waited three months in another camp for another boat. During this delay, we met up there in that camp with Zsenka Festinger, the eldest of the Festinger sisters, and Johnny Festinger, their brother, who had also survived the Japanese concentration camps.

EDITH: Soon after leaving Radio Munich, although I wasn't looking for work, I met someone from UNRRA that was looking for people that spoke English and who had come from the camps. United Nations Relief and Rehabilitation Administration came about before the United Nations was established.[40] And that's how the next job happened. I went to work for UNRRA. You see, I really was looking for something more interesting and meaningful. It was the most interesting job. Also, during this time I actually worked for three agencies: UNRRA, JDC, and HIAS. They kept borrowing me back and forth. Like loaning me out. They also hired my sister Hilda. We wore American uniforms and I had my own office.[41]

HILDA: We decided we were going to work for HIAS, a Jewish American organization, that gave us jobs in the office connected with the UNRRA. The beautiful part of this was helping the displaced people. We were in contact with the American Consulate. We were dressed in the American Army uniform, with the UNRRA insignia on the jacket. We were, at least I speak for myself, so proud that from then on, the Germans were frightened of us! This being achieved, we hoped not to have another terrible experience on the tram.

MENDI: In the meantime Hilda and Edith changed their jobs, and went to work for HIAS, and I got a job there, too. One day a very young boy that I had known came to me there at HIAS. He could have been thirteen then and I recognized him. He was a shtuberdeenz. A main Kapo from one of our barracks, who was in charge of about eight hundred people, was a German criminal and he had that young boy with him during that time. The shtuberdeenz made him coffee or tea. And the Kapo also used the little boy for sexual purposes. He was quite bad to that boy. The boy came with his uncle to register at HIAS, and I recognized him. I told the uncle that his nephew was a bad boy. The uncle begged me to forgive him. He said, "Look, that child was eight years old when he went into the concentration camp and a miracle happened, and he survived. He had been in camps for four or five years." And so I forgave him. And they went to America. That is where I also ran into Herschowitz, trying to emigrate. Later on I heard that Herschowitz spent some time in prison in Romania.

EDITH: People were waiting to be interviewed by me and they were standing in line all the way up the street, and I had a doorman that wouldn't let anyone in. And then I was interviewing these people and helping them fill out affidavits to the states or countries wherever they hoped to go to.

In between all those interviews, I had to also denazify every one I spoke with. I had to ask them all kinds of questions to find out where they were at a certain date, to sort out their Nazi affiliations and criminal history. Everybody was Jewish in those days, if you know what I mean. Those were the ones trying to say that they were Jewish, and then the interviews became interrogations and they failed because they weren't even in concentration camps. They were trying to fake it. If someone that I was interviewing was pretending to be Jewish, I could find out. If they said they were Jewish and I had the notion that they were not, I would inject a few Jewish words and then they couldn't climb out of that. And they could have an accent, a German accent. Or they could say they were from another country, like Romania but they didn't speak the language, and I did.

And every day I was speaking to several ambassadors from different countries that were positioned in Munich at that time. And also, these people that came in didn't speak English, and sometimes they didn't speak Hungarian either. So whatever language they spoke, I translated. Even if it was a language that I didn't speak, like Polish, if they were really Jews then they spoke Yiddish, the Jewish language, which I also understand. I speak five languages altogether. So all daylong I was filling out forms, using a typewriter, filing, and doing a lot of telephoning to the ambassadors. We had to communicate with the ambassadors so much because of the quotas. The quotas for emigration were very small and they depended on the country that you were born in.

I loved this job, but there were some problems there at UNRRA. I had somebody above me and he was a married man who lied about being married. One day he invited me to go to the park and bring the typewriter along. He was an American Captain. I went to the park with him, thinking we were going to just work. Then he told me that he wanted to go out with me. I told him that I was engaged because at that time I already knew Nate. Then my boss told me that if I refused to go out with him he would see to it that I never would get to Australia. That is where I had to go if I couldn't marry Nate. In the times that we are in now, this would be called sexual harassment. In those days it was very common, I think. So, this guy, he never got near me, but he was after me tremendously. Later on when it got to the point where he found out that I was truly engaged to Nate, then he laid low, because he knew I was dating an American.

And then there was corruption, like theft going on in UNRRA during that time, but I am not going to tell you names, I just know for a fact that huge packages were supposed to be donated away to us, to people like me, and a lot of this stuff was confiscated by the workers that worked there. I mean these were American people that were supposed to take care of us, and supply stuff to everybody like me. I don't really know what they did with it; I just knew that there was a shortage there.

Hilda and I had our positions working for the UNRRA and we were well taken care of. In addition to supplying us with uniforms, we also had a PX card.[42] We were able to go there and buy all the things that we needed, just like the GIs. But we worried about the other survivors. It was disappointing to think that the people you have put your trust in could be ripping you off.[43]

And also, look at what happened with the U.S. Army stealing all of the Hungarian property. Have you heard of the Hungarian Gold Train?[44] All of our possessions that had been confiscated by the Germans was eventually found and stolen by American soldiers. We didn't know that at the time.

EDITH: My relationship with Nate was different than any courtships with the other GIs. Nate was unlike the others. Even though John Lury was charismatic, Nate was more of an extrovert. Nate was very friendly to everyone: it didn't matter who they were. He was always ready to entertain; so outgoing, lively, and sociable. John was more of an introvert. They were opposites in that way. Whereas Nate would bring things, gifts of food and coal. John sent things, like that time he sent his footman.

The first thing that surprised me about Nate was that he was wearing a bomber's jacket; you know the kind of leather jacket the fliers wear? That impressed me. That and that he was driving the Jeep, and GIs didn't have Jeeps unless they were driving a Captain, or somebody with a title. And he was so self-secure, self-confident. He knew what he was doing and where he was going.

There was another thing, Nate didn't go at me. That really opened my eyes, you know and it felt like he respected me. He wasn't aggressively trying to kiss me. At first he went after Hilda because he said that I was a little wild. I think I was too good looking. It was my eyes; he told me I had dancing eyes.

And anyhow, from then on, he started being very wonderful to my friends. You know, always showering us with all kinds of things. My cousin Janka Festinger was getting married to Bob Speace, a GI, and Nate took care of the whole party. He brought the food, the chickens, and everything. He threw a whole big catered reception. Janka and Bob spent their honeymoon night in the little white bedroom in my apartment.

That little bedroom was like a mesmerizing thing. There was one giant window and just a white bed in the room, there wasn't anything much there except the bed. The window looked out onto the street, to the other buildings. You could see people walking by and the entire hustle bustle of the city. It was just very, very nice and warm. Whoever slept there must have known that they were out having a good time, in a welcoming area.

I can't really explain what it was, I just started loving Nate! I suppose Nate's good personality had a lot to do with it. When I was with him I could be myself. I was comfortable with Nate. One time the window was open, it was at night, and he was over by the fireplace and then he had lain down. It had been a very warm day and he had his shirt off and the moon was shining on his chest, you know, and when I saw that I fell in love with him. I just didn't tell him. I didn't. I had my eyes on him. It felt permanent-like, so I thought to myself, I'd better hold back and play a little bit hard to get. And I guess from then on I somehow felt that I was belonging to him. The two of us were completely one.

During this time I was still dating John Lury. I was in love with both of them. You think that's impossible? If you can love two children, why couldn't you love two men? The timing was bad, because when Nate started taking me out, I was already going around with Doctor John Lury. Nate knew that I was out with John and he always came around at night. Nate was friends with my brother Mendi and my sister Hilda, and so he would go to sleep in the little white bedroom.

And on one occasion, during this time period I was out with the doctor. John had taken me to the Sea House, the officers' club. It wasn't that Nate was at my apartment the entire evening waiting. I don't know where he was all evening; he didn't arrive until eleven o'clock because he knew I was busy. I couldn't just cut it off with the doctor and I didn't want to. And Nate did not ask me to end it with John. No, he didn't. He was not that type. If he was jealous I never knew it. I think that was intriguing.

John Lury had a friend, another doctor, and he was dating Hilda. And the two guys went to Nuremberg when they were all done in the Army. He was already gone for a couple of weeks, and then suddenly one day he showed up with his friend just to see me again one more time. He had somebody drive him. My feelings for John, well, I was glad to see him. But I was already engaged; I didn't have to question anything. When John learned that I was engaged to Nate, he didn't say a word. Nothing. He did not ask me to leave Nate. I couldn't help but wondering if maybe he was already married. I didn't know why the guy didn't try to marry me.[45] I couldn't figure it out! I probably would have married John during the time that Nate disappeared on me.

HILDA: Nate was waiting patiently until John Lury was discharged from the Army. There was another one that was after Edith. Abe Green was his name. Edith was very popular with lots of admirers. Edith became enamored with Nate. I thought it was a joke, not serious. She liked several American GIs. So did I!

EDITH: Abe Green knew that I was going around with Nate. On the night that I got engaged to Nate, that was when Abe cried his eyes out. The guy went to pieces, and I lost respect for him. I was just an innocent girl and he acted like it was a tragedy, like his whole world would collapse. It was too much for me; I couldn't handle the guilt that he was putting on me. Just because his sister sent me a package? Did I owe him something? The guy had asked me if I needed anything, and I happened to have needed a pair of shoes. Nothing wrong with that. I had just gotten through with the concentration camp.

I didn't feel anything wrong with accepting a package from some American Jews that wanted to help me. It wasn't fair to put that responsibility on me. I was still raw from everything that I suffered. I felt something was wrong with his behavior. It frightened me, I remember that.

Nate and I went everywhere together in Munich, driving in his Jeep, sightseeing. Like I said, Nate was the only GI that I knew that had a Jeep. Nate was a born leader, which was so attractive to me. He was absolutely a big shot in the area because of his position at the Cool House, the American food supply business.

Mostly we all went to the Lowenbrau Keller, where the Jews were gathering. We wanted to be with Jewish people, and we met everybody there. Besides the Sea House, the nightlife and social life for us in Munich really centered on the Lowenbrau Keller. We went there almost every night. All I ever could, I was there! Well, for instance, weekends for sure. There was no music; it was too crowded for that but we didn't care. It was just a wonderful feeling for everybody, all of us Jews, to feel the freedom, to see everybody. Free! It was just a joy. It's very difficult to explain. Right now I can close my eyes and feel just like I am sitting in the Keller. I remember the stairway; you go up the stairs to go out.

NATE: I want to tell the story about that time in Munich when Edith and Hilda got arrested. I'll tell you what happened, but you'd better keep this part quiet! My friends and I pretended to be civilians working for the Army. We got false papers and I.D. buttons so we could go to the nightclubs.

HILDA: It was curfew time for civilians to be off the street at night. We returned with Nate and Howard at twelve at night. The American Military Police stopped the Jeep and took Edith and me to the German jail overnight. It was catastrophic! We tried to tell them that Edith was engaged to an American GI and I was with his friend from the nightclub and we were on our way to go home, but it seemed that the boys didn't know the law. You can imagine Edith and I were not aware of it.

EDITH: There was one night that began beautifully and then became a nightmare. It was in Munich and there was curfew, and civilians were not supposed to be on the streets after a certain time. I was out on a date with Nate, Hilda was with Howard Spear. At that time Nate had borrowed an outfit, a uniform. You see, he was bothered by the fact that I was going out to the Sea House with my boyfriend, the doctor. This was really before Nate and I had become engaged to be married. Nate was jealous that I had been dancing at the Officers Club with John Lury, so he got the uniform he needed to get into the Sea House, and we stayed out dancing at the club until after curfew. And then Hilda and I got arrested!

HILDA: Edith and I were squeezed in a cell with the rest of the girls and were standing up all night. Next morning the Warden ordered us to scrub the floor. Of course we refused. We said to her, "We were kneeling and persecuted in Auschwitz, we don't obey these orders!"

EDITH: Nate and Howard went back to their barracks and slept. We were outrageously upset! The Germans that arrested us told my sister and me that a doctor was going to have to inspect us, as they thought that we were prostitutes.

NATE: The goddamn Germans; they worked for us. They said that the girls were whores with syphilis. You can imagine how angry I was.

EDITH: In the morning, the Warden said to us, "The doctor is going to examine both of you." I tried to make a deal with the doctor, because my sister and I had never slept with a man before. I said to him, "If you examine me and find out that I am telling him the truth, would you please let us go?" And he said, "No, you both are to be examined." And he took a long instrument, like a needle and pushed it down my pena. The doctor did whatever it took to find out if we were virgins or not. And we were. And luckily he did not break us, that German bastard of a doctor. I don't know when Nate and Howard had come back to the jail but when they did, they had a U.S. Army Captain with them. And there was such a terrible stink going on, a big deal; they were hollering and yelling, and so we were released.

NATE: Howard and I demanded to see the person in charge. We went upstairs to see the American colonel. Then the German officer came up and said there had been a mistake. He said, "These girls are virgins." A doctor had been called in to physically examine the girls. The girls were very upset. We all were. But we all got over it.

HILDA: The same morning was the court order—a terrible performance—the jail doctor had to examine us. We cried and refused, we said, "We are virgins." We felt very embarrassed to be examined. He pronounced that he wouldn't hurt us. In the courtroom were Nate and Howard, waiting for us to be released. The American judge said that I had to remain in the jail because I had a disease.

I was hysterical. I said again, "I am a virgin!" The American judge ordered the doctor in who examined us, because actually he had congratulated us for being innocent girls. So the doctor testified that I had been mixed up with a German woman. The American judge apologized to Nate and Howard for this horrible mistake and embarrassment. They released me. They handed us over to Nate and Howard and we went home. What a horrible experience after our miraculous freedom from Auschwitz and the rest.

EDITH: When Nate and I were together we did a lot of talking. Mostly he asked me about way back in Hungary, how it was. I know when I felt that he was very close to me because one night at the apartment on Ganghofer Strasse, we were sitting in a big chair. I was sitting on his lap and the fire was going and he was asking me about my life and I was telling him about everything.

I told Nate all of my stories. I told him the story about the Angora rabbit farm in Satu-Mare; that was one thing that made me get so emotional, and I put my head on his shoulder and I was just crying bitterly and he was holding me trying to appease me. I felt very, very close to him then. And when he kissed me I knew he loved me, that night I knew. But then, after that night, I wasn't sure if he loved me or not. I never would have believed that he would marry me. He never actually said the words, 'Will you marry me?' He just came right out and said, "I'm taking you home with me." That's what he said. And he told me stories about his life back home and what he did, that he and his family owned a lumberyard. He told me about his parents, that they came from Russia and they, too had fled persecution. We had something very much in common. And I think he was testing me about being Jewish and what I am like, and what my parents were like. So I told him all the stories. He told me that he had grown up on a farm. I couldn't imagine that. I wasn't very impressed with that because in those days, back in Hungary, Jewish people rarely ran agricultural farms. Then after that one night, he told me that he had written to his father and mother. I said, "What did you write to them?" And he told me that he explained all about me, where I had come from and my background and my parents. So we got kind of closer together, like that.

KURT: In February 1946, a British transport ship finally came for us in Jakarta. There were fifteen hundred people on board and it took thirty days to arrive in Holland. The night before we arrived, they showed a movie on the ship and announced that telegrams had arrived for some people. I was so shocked when my name was called out. I couldn't understand who in the world would be contacting us! At that point we didn't know that any other relatives had survived in Europe, from the Holocaust. It was my other sister in Holland saying that she was alive, that she had survived Auschwitz. She wanted us to know that she had an apartment ready for us in Amsterdam.

NATE: It wasn't until sometime in March of 1946, while we were in Munich, that a little German boy working for the Dutch underground smuggling mail showed up at the girls' apartment with a letter saying that Edith's sister Piri and her husband Kurt

Meyers were alive. They and their two children had survived Japanese concentration camps in the Dutch East Indies and were now in Holland. Soon after getting that news, I headed home to Michigan through La Harve, France. I got on a ship. A smart aleck Lieutenant who was in charge of the men on the ship detained me. He didn't like me. He wanted to arrest me for desertion, which is another story that I can't tell! So in order to get away from the Lieutenant, I volunteered for kitchen duty under the captain on the ship. The captain ordered me not to give the officers special food. The captain sheltered me.

I got an honorable discharge; it was issued at Camp Atterbury, Indiana on April 20, 1946.[46] I went back to Michigan but planned to arrange for Edith to follow me or I would come back for her in thirty days. Howard Spear stayed on in Munich as a civilian working for the Army. I wrote and telegraphed through my friend Howard to Edith. There was a lot of red tape. It ended up taking a lot longer than I had thought to bring Edith over to the States. The War Bride's Law had not yet been passed. The new law said that if a GI married in Europe he could bring a war bride back on his passport. I didn't get back to Europe until July 1946 for my bride.

EDITH: Up until March 1946, when Nate had to leave to go back to the States without me, there was all kinds of activity going on then because he got in touch with all the agencies and where I worked. He knew that my family in Australia was sending me a Landing Permit; that's what you needed to get there. I was supposed to go there with my brother Mendi and my sister, Hilda. I told

Nate, "If you leave me in Munich, I am just going to go ahead and go to Australia. I don't believe that you will come back for me."

He said that he was making all the arrangements for my entry to America and if it didn't work, he would come back for me. A lot of GIs went back to America and they never came back. A lot of GIs were liars. They said that they were coming back, or didn't mention they were married. I didn't know if Nate was truly coming back for me. I couldn't really believe him and he wasn't the type of person that would tell you stories to endear you or anything like that.

I was wondering why he didn't marry me before he left to go home. Maybe that is part of the reason I didn't believe that he was coming back for me. Or maybe there were certain regulations against him getting married. Although my cousin Janka Festinger had already married an American GI. I don't remember if Bob Speace was allowed to take her out of Europe, since the War Bride Law had not yet been passed. I don't remember much about the time leading up to Nate's departure. I didn't have much time to remember his leaving because in my mind, he wasn't mine at all, still. I didn't believe that he was coming back for me. And I was busy working and carrying on with my life. I am the type of person that doesn't cry over lost things; I just carry on with my life. A survivor, yes, that's me. When Nate left, I did not make it a memory link in my mind. To me, the minute he left, I said goodbye to him and that is exactly how I felt. I never thought I would see him again. I didn't know if I would have a future at all. I was aware of some of his efforts. Even with all of the documentation, the affidavits and cables, all the things that he was putting together so that he could marry me and bring me back to the U.S.A., I had hope, but truly still didn't believe it.[47]

HILDA: Nate was discharged from the army and he went back to America. Edith, Mendi, and I had gone through the investigations about people like us and we had applied for affidavits to go the U.S.A. We went through the Consulate. Everything was finalized; it was only a matter of time when we shall be called up with the affidavits, and we were the very first ones to receive it. In the meantime, our sister, Helen and her husband Jules had fixed everything for us to come to Australia. They also paid the fares for us. So Mendi, Edith, and I all decided to go to Australia instead of America.

EDITH: In the meantime, the correspondence between Nate and me continued, from Munich, Germany to Mount Clemens, Michigan. Howard Spear was very involved in helping to get the mail and many telegrams back and forth. Hilda and Howard were still dating. I wrote many letters to Nate and to his parents during this time, all of which he saved. Some of Nate's letters that he wrote to me were very steamy. I remember in one letter he told me about a dream that he had about me. He wrote that he woke up in a sweat. I can't tell you any more about those letters. It just wouldn't be right. He saved one letter that he wrote to me with instructions on applying for Visas and he included some more affidavits, which were used to vouch for his support of me.

It wasn't working out that I would be able to go to America on my own. He wanted to be able to just send for me. But that was not meant to be.

Munich March 10, 1946
Naty dear!

I try my best to keep myself strong until the day I will see you again. Every night I go to bed, with tears in my eyes. I talk to your picture and kiss it a thousand times. Sometimes I feel I get crazy of the thought that I will see you again, and have you for always.

I wish I could see your dear parents' faces when they first saw you. Is your dear father better now?

We are still around Munich, and I think for another month or two, now my sister Aranka is coming here from Roumania, so I don't feel so bad for staying here a little longer.[48]

I was to see the French Consul, but the papers didn't come yet. The man though showed me the first news from Holland, sent us my sister Piri's address so we can write her and ask her to fix a visa for us to get to Holland.

Darling I can still hear you saying: It won't be long - - - - I wish I could be near your home somewhere right now, just to watch your dear parents how they must be. They really need it after such a long waiting. It is 11:30 right now. Hilda and Howard came back just now from the Sea House; they look so happy, I am glad for that.

Mendi is kidding around with me and he teases me all the time. He says, "You can't go to dance anymore; you have to be a good girl." I am really good, but nobody knows why, they don't know my dear secret, that I am all the time with you, no matter where I am or what time it is you are always near me, that's something that I can't explain to you on paper. If you feel the same maybe you will understand me without those poor words, which might sound like a sentimental poem.

Be good Nately and don't forget your promise…I love you dearly and will never stop loving you.

Forever your Edith

P.S. These are the pictures we took near your house.

Munich 13 March 1946

My dearest Nate!

Yesterday I once more was to see the French Consul, without any success. I talked to Mr. Prohlick (Siebertstrasse.) He promised he will call Paris to hear how the papers are going along. I don't know the answer yet, as I was told, many people are waiting for papers to get to France, which was started much more before ours.

The first D.P. transport will begin on the 26 April next month with 900 Jewish DPs, all which has the affidavits to America. I want to hope that we won't have to wait very long.

I am in the little room right now, that is the only place I am not disturbed by anybody. The day you left I felt so unhappy. Nobody was in the house, everything was so quiet and I prayed to God to return you home to your dear parents. Nate dear kiss your dear mother for me and tell her I love her like I loved my own mother.

Please dear; write to me as often as you can, I would be very happy to hear how things are going along.

Howard is coming to us often, when he brought me your letter, before he gave it to me he asked if I was a good girl and he closed my eyes and put the letters in my hand. I was so happy I had to give him a big kiss (on his face!).

Next week maybe I will go to Garmisch with Hilda for a few days.[49] Nate dear I wish I could be with you. I miss you so much. Goodbye till tomorrow, then I write you again.

I love you Nate

Forever your Edith

Mount Clemens, Michigan
April 25-1946
My Darling Editke,
I love you. Here is a snap of my younger brother Emanuel and me.
   I love you
   Nately

Munich 8 May 1946
Dear Nate!
   I was very surprised reading your letter. Please Naty try to understand. I know you do your best to get the papers for all three of us. But Nate you forgot one thing. If my papers will be ready before my sister and brother I will have to leave alone. If the American Consul is calling me telling that I have to be ready for transportation I can't tell them to leave me here for longer. I work for the HIAS as interviewer and I am clear with the possibilities of emigrations. The Australian quota is filled till June. So I don't have any hope to leave till after July maybe August if I am lucky.
   Yesterday I got some mail from Holland, Roumania and Australia. My sister and brother from East India are already in Australia and feel very happy that we are alive.[50] My brother is engaged to a girl from India, which is right now in Holland with her father… our boat to Australia is leaving in maximum two months, they have a copy of our Landing Permits if they are needed they can send them to us. Before two days we had a letter from Mr. Mark London, he was writing to us very good news. But as America is in consideration right now we don't bother yet with Australia. If I ask a transit visa for Hilda and Emanuel (Mendi), we can't travel in the same time. That is why I asked you for that cable I got today.
   Every Jew living in U.S. Zone can register himself for America with a cable or letter from some relative in the U.S.A., which states an affidavit. I am very busy these days, and as I have so many friends, they don't forget to find me some work all the time. But I do it with pleasure; somebody has

to help them, that is why I wanted this job. Next week I will be clothed in uniform which idea is not too bad here in Germany.

I am writing to you from the office, hope you don't mind if I close now, I have some more papers to file. Till the next letter

Thousand kisses from Edith

P.S. My Jewish name is: Etya Sosa[51]

Please dear Nate give my kind regards and kisses to your dearest Mother and Father and regards to Emanuel.

MENDI: From Germany I had corresponded with Jules and Helenke, my brother-in-law and my sister in Sydney. By May of 1946, my brother Johnny and our oldest sister Zsenka were already in Australia. They had arrived from Singapore, Indonesia fresh out of the Japanese concentration camps. Some of the family from Indonesia went to Holland and some came to Australia.

I knew about Australia and that it was famous for its wool and its sheep and I had that idea of going into Angora wool, to introduce Angora wool in Australia, because it was very fashionable at that time, all over Europe. I had that love for animals and I thought of breeding thousands of Angora rabbits again. That was what I had written to my brother-in-law about, my idea of making a business out of this.

Jules bought a farm with forty acres near Windsor, a placed called Freeman's Reach before I arrived. He also had bought all the rabbit cages, which I had written to him about.

Mount Clemens, Michigan
Western Union telegram May 1946
DEAR HOWARD
PLEASE CONVEY TO EDITH FESTINGER THAT AFFIDAVITS HAVE BEEN
SENT TO THE AMERICAN CONSUL SEPARATELY ONE FOR EDITH
AND ONE FOR HILDA AND EMANUEL FESTINGER ARRANGE TO
CALL ME BY PHONE MOUNT CLEMENS 2673 AFTER MAY SEVENTH
ANYTIME HAVE EDITH WITH YOU
LOVE NATHAN

Munich 8 May 1946
Dearest Father!

I was very glad to hear that you are much better now.

I feel happy that you and the dear Mother are loving me before
seeing me. If I would thank you, it would be something very simple. There
is about two years passed from the day I lost my dearest parents. As I was
very young and unhappy I was sure I won't love anybody else as much as
I did love them. And now I don't understand myself. I miss you very much
and wish to kiss you both and have that feeling I missed for two years.
As I am not a too bad girl I hope you will like me a little if you see me in
person. With the best wishes for the dear mother and you dear Father.

All my love and kisses Edith

Munich 9 May 1946
My dearest Nate!

Just a few lines to let you know that the registration papers for
emigration that I have written you about are already at the American
Consul. As the Roumanian quota is very small and already filled up till July
I am afraid we will have to wait longer.

How are you darling? I got your pictures; the one with Emanuel is
very sweet. I wish I could see you, I feel so lonely, but I am strong and
don't cry too much. You are very optimistic, darling, if you think that in 4-6
weeks I will be with you. It is not so easy as you dream it. There are many
hundreds and thousands of people having the affidavit for a long time

and still can't travel yet. As you see dear, some people are lucky. I showed your cable by the HIAS where I work. They said I don't have to worry about cables and affidavits because they fixed a corporate affidavit for us. The consul has to give us just the visa.... Later on everything stopped. The Consul has ordered that we cannot make any more registrations. There are too many people for transportation.

That is about all for today. Thanks to your dear Father for taking care of you. Hope you are a good boy.

It is funny that you want me to write you every day. How about you? Do I see good exchanges? Mail from America arrives in four days. Why don't you write to me more often? Don't tell me stories that you are very busy. If you are as busy as I imagine still you can let me know in a few lines how is everything and if you still love me.

Till the next letter
Love and kisses
From your Edith

Munich 17th of May 1946
Darling!

Before a few days I wrote to you a long letter in the same time to your parents. Howard was not here in those days so I sent the letters to Howard through the German mail. He is here now, and sorry he didn't get the letters. Honey, I feel fine the only trouble is that it will be long, maybe many months till we will get some transportation.

Hope you are all well. I love you darling and wish I could be with you very soon.

Love and kisses to your parents.
Be good and don't forget about your Edith

Munich May 26, 1946
My dear Nate!

I got the Landing Permits through Daily, who was in France and came back before a few days.

I still don't know anything about our emigration. The Roumanian quota will be opened in July and if we will have the chance to leave, I don't know yet. I try everything possible to get out, and work even with the Landing Permits, which might help us to get out sooner. If leaving with the permits, we might go first to France and from there I do not know how the HIAS will arrange the transportation for us. Our applications for emigrating to USA as I told you are by the American Consul with the corporate affidavits which the HIAS gave for us.

Hilda and myself are dressed with the American uniform and have all the right to go into GI places or any other places where civilians can't go. We can get everything in the P.X. and have A.P.O. address. I will make some pictures and will send you.

Darling, I miss you very much but "God" knows when I will see you again. I can't do anything in this matter. The day I know something new about it I will send you a cable.

Darling why don't you write to me often? You are very bad to me.

All my love and kisses

Your Edith

Munich June 3rd 1946

My dearest Nate!

…I am glad to write you some good news, we are called by the CIC to clear some questions; and as many people are waiting for this for two, three months, it came very suddenly.[52] That doesn't mean that we will leave in 3-4 weeks, but it won't be so long as I thought. On July 15th a boat is leaving from France for Australia, our director of HIAS could arrange our transportation to France, but as I wrote you once I don't want to go to Australia, I don't care what anybody says, I will wait even longer if I have to. I love you Nate.

Forever your Edith

P.S. Write to my address to HIAS where I work.

EDITH: As I still didn't actually believe Nate was coming back for me, Hilda, Mendi, and I were ready to go to Paris. There was a cable that Nate sent to Howard Spear saying something like, "Stop Edith in Paris, I am on my way."

That's what he told me but I didn't believe him. I will tell you how I didn't believe it: We got ready to take a train to Paris, my sister, brother and I, where they sent some of the Jewish people in order to go to different countries to carry on with their lives. I was headed for Australia. I went to Paris with the idea that I was going to carry on with my life. I had quit my job with UNRRA by this time. I was very happy to quit because the guy that was my boss had become very mean. He kept threatening me that I am never going to get to Australia. I can't remember his name, he was a son of a bitch and I hated him. If I could remember his name, I would tell the world how he harassed me!

Mount Clemens, Michigan
June 7, 1946
My Darling Edith-

I am writing you again because I love you and want to be near you even if just by mail. So far I don't know what is happening. But it seems you have applied for Transit Visas. NOW LISTEN: <u>if you have applied for Transit Visas to America and they have been refused, take these papers and affidavits which I now send to you and apply for a visitor visa. Because you want to come to visit your fiancé. Remember don t use these papers unless your Transit Visa has been refused.</u> A Transit Visa is a permit to stop in America for a little while and then go on to Australia. Please write to me soon and let me know when you receive these papers. Also please try to call me. We are trying many different ways to make arrangements. And one of them will work. So be good because I am true to you. I love you Honey and it won't be long before I show you that I do.
Love, Nate

Chapter Seven

Finally it became obvious to Nate that he could not get Edith to America on her own, and he made plans to return to Europe. Nate Litvin departed from the Detroit Willow Run Airport for New York on July 4, 1946. He flew from La Guardia Airport in New York on July 5, destination Paris, with a stop in Amsterdam. He wasn't sure if Edith had received the telegram that he sent to her in Munich. Edith had sent a cable to Nate telling him that she was leaving Munich for Paris on July 2, and mentioned that she may be in Marseille, to look for her there, and find the address through HIAS. She wasn't sure if Nate had received her cable. Nate had arrived in Paris on July 7, 1946 and checked into the Hotel Francia. On July 8 he went to the HIAS office looking for the Festingers, had lunch and looked for some soap, as there was no soap at the Francia. On July 10 he cabled his parents expressing worry that he was unable to call Munich and find Edith. Then he went to U.S. Military Headquarters seeking permission to use their telephone. He was able to make the call to Munich and get the news that Edith would arrive that day. He got a room at the California Hotel and then he went to the train station and awaited the Orient Express coming from Munich. He spotted the Festingers coming down the steps. He saw his beloved Edith and in the next moment she was in his arms.

❧

EDITH: It was time to pack up the apartment, except we just left it. Everything went so smooth because I didn't have much. I didn't have many clothes to pack. I had a suitcase by then. But all I had was a couple of blouses that Miki had made for me out of parachutes, and some underwear. Because we had to give all the UNRRA uniforms back, I had very little clothing. All of my photos and papers were packed, all of my new memories.

There is something important that I need to clear up. It has to do with when I arrived in Paris on the train. And I did not believe that Nate was coming back for me. It appears that all of the telegrams that he sent to me should have convinced me that he was coming back for me. I think that I can explain that to you simply. This business of me believing or not believing about him coming back and taking me to his home, it was always a matter of whether two people believed in the same thing. Nate believed that he was coming back. And I, with all the other Jews, believing that nobody is coming back at all. Here we were stuck in the strange goddamn country of Germany and the words that Nate would think or prove in a letter, was up in the air. It wasn't anything that constituted proof that he was ever going to take me back there.

And then the three of us Festingers got on the train, The Orient Express.[53] Elegant. First Class. Everybody could have a room of their own with a separate bathroom and a porter fixing our beds for the night. But Hilda and I wanted to share a room. And then the party just started. It was the most gorgeous time that I ever had in my whole life. I was free, I didn't have anybody, my boyfriend had left, and I was headed for Australia.

HILDA: Edith and Mendi were very excited at that stage to come to Australia. As Edith, Mendi, and I were traveling to Paris from Munich, we enjoyed every minute of the trip.

EDITH: That overnight train trip on the Orient Express was magical! I just met one person that I liked very much. He was a GI headed for a vacation in Paris and we were sitting in our private room. There were two beds there, you know, vis-à-vis, and Hilda was in the room, too. She was sitting with one GI and I was sitting with the other and we were having a wonderful time. We were laughing! They had brought a couple of drinks for themselves from the bar there, in the dining car. And they bought us seltzer and Coca-Cola. And they wined us and dined us in the dining car. And he and I were kissing. When I got to Paris, my lips were puffy, all swollen from kissing him all night. We were up all night long.

And in the morning when we arrived, and the doors opened, guess who was there waiting for me? I saw Nate when I started coming down the steps. The guy I was with was holding my hand. I had to just quickly say goodbye to him, good night to him and thank him for the good time but had to say, "My fiancé is waiting for me right down the steps!" The guy was flabbergasted. And I quickly ran down the steps and there was Nate! I flew right into his arms! I was so surprised. Shocked! And so very happy. Very! I couldn't believe that my dreams were actually coming true. And he took us to the Hotel California where he had a room ready. We all stayed in one room, the four of us. And he brought me the most gorgeous nightgown with a robe to match for our wedding, our future wedding.

HILDA: While we were still on the Orient Express, suddenly I said to Edith, "I have a strong feeling that Nate will be in Paris Railway Station surprising you," and that is how it was.

I don't remember how Edith felt, but as for Mendi, and myself, we were very unhappy. After what we went through, Edith and I totally, strictly, had promised never to be separated. If you know what is means to be hurt and disappointed in a love affair, well it was much worse than that. In normal times and circumstances it would have been different. But it was not a normal situation. The way I felt losing my parents was very tragic but losing Edith to Nate was horrific. I suffered a long time. I was immature, you may say. This is how I felt.

MENDI: After six months in Germany, my two sisters and I went to Paris. I remember the time we were on the Munich train platform in Paris: Edith, Hilda, and I traveled from Munich to Paris.

We had first class sleeping compartments, slept all night and arrived in the morning in Paris. Nate surprised us by waiting at the station in Paris. He told us he had special permission from General Eisenhower to travel from the United States to Paris to take his future bride home.

EDITH: That first day in Paris in July 1946, what Nate wanted to show us right away when we first arrived, was a bakery. The French make these long, long breads called baguettes, that look like a yard long and he bought two for each of us and we put those under our arms. And then we sat down on some outdoor benches and we were chewing on the bread.

It was wonderful! Nate had a small bottle of wine with him. So, he took it out of his pocket and we all had a sip of it. We made a toast, "L'Chaim, to life and to freedom, and to love!"

And then we went straight to the California Hotel. I couldn't wait to greet my fiancé the way I was supposed to greet him; I couldn't do that on the street. The hotel suited me just fine. Nate hailed a cab. He flagged down the French taxi. He didn't have a Jeep anymore. He was out of the Army then. I'll tell you something; I was very shocked to see him in civilian clothes. He must have gained about thirty pounds at home eating his mother's cooking. I was shocked. But of course, I still loved him; even though he was a little heavier it didn't make any difference! He was the same man, just without the uniform.

The California Hotel, from a distance looking in, was very, very in the past century. Actually, it looked like the eighteenth century, not even nineteenth. In those hotels, all the closets were out, armoires and furniture that you can push around. And you hung your clothes in those things, but I didn't have a problem because I had so few clothes with me. But I did have a beautiful coat that Miki had made for me for the trip. She made it out of a blanket. It was gorgeous, sky blue! One for Hilda and one for me. Nate had brought a movie camera with him when he came back to Europe. In the movies as we are coming down the steps at the horse races in Paris, you can see the two blue coats on us. By the way it was very exciting because the horse races in Paris were the most famous in all of Europe. It was my first time going to any horse races and it was a novelty for me.

At the California Hotel we had a beautiful room. This is what we did; there were two beds apart from each other and every night Mendi and Nate took the mattresses off and put them on the floor, so we had four beds for us to sleep on. Everything else was downstairs. Like the restaurant, very French, very marvelous. We had Hilda and Mendi as our chaperones, which was beautiful. I didn't mind at all.

I have to tell you something really interesting. My first time that I went downstairs in the restaurant, right after we had arrived, we were being shown to our table, and guess who was sitting at the next table? It was the Major that was my boss at the UNRRA. Can you imagine that bastard being there? Yes, it was him. That was who was sitting right there with his ugly wife. I told Nate. He said that I should just ignore it. So I did. Believe me, it was a big punishment for him to see me there with my fiancé. At that point, he knew he couldn't stop me from going to Australia anymore, because I was on my way to America. Can you imagine the coincidence?

We sat down to lunch and had the most wonderful meal. They had the most gorgeous French salad that you could ever have seen in your life. They serve a salad completely different than the American salad. Everything sliced and the gorgeous gravy all over it, beautiful. Oh, and I want to tell you about the concierge at the hotel. Nate introduced me to him, in French, and told him that I was his fiancée.[54]

What was going on with us in France, and what we were doing during the days was not all about sightseeing. There was a lot of paperwork to be taken care of and it took a lot of time. There were all the offices that we had to visit to take care of our journey forward. We were also running around in connection with Hilda and Mendi's traveling, to arrive in Sydney, Australia. It was very difficult.

Nate and I had all kinds of instructions to follow in order to get our French marriage license. We had to get officially translated instructions. It was very confusing. We had to go to the two Romanian Embassies because there was no actual record of where I was born. All of the certificates stating who I was were made up by the Jewish organizations to give people like me, that were liberated, an identity.

Nate was very wonderful. He was relentless to get all of the business taken care of in order to get our civil marriage ceremony arranged. Some of the offices that we had to go to were only open a few hours per day. There was a lot of back and forth running around. The problem with the civil marriage ceremony was the fact that I was born in Romania and I had no way to prove it. And finally the French officials got in touch with Romania for the proof.

I was actually born in Romania, but then that part of Romania became Hungary. It was a confusing state of existence, really, to explain to people of why I am considered Hungarian and Romanian. Really, where I lived in Transylvania, it was the Romanians and Hungarians that were feuding all the time and so in the First World War that area was Hungary. And then when the First War ended in 1918, the Romanians were fighting again with the Hungarians and they took the territory over and then I was born after that.

MENDI: Hilda and I were not able to get a visa to travel to Australia. Nate and Edith traveled with us from Paris to Marseille, to go to the Romanian Consulate, hoping to get a visa there but we could not get it.

EDITH: We took a train to Marseille in order to go to the Romanian Consulate there. It was quite a long ride; it took seven hours. Oh, and an American GI paid for our dinner on the train. We had run out of American dollars. That was really something. Oh, and when we arrived in Marseille, you should have seen the mosquitoes from being on the water. Marseille is a gorgeous, beautiful city by the ocean. Did you know that all that water that surrounds Marseille is like the ocean kissing it? They have all the ports where all the big ships are arriving from all over the world. And all the people that were out fishing on the boats were doing a lot of singing at the same time! There was accordion playing going on. And on little boats there were a lot of young people, young men with girls that looked romantically involved. I had a good time. My brother and sister also had business in Marseille. They were with us. We went everywhere together. We were always together. We had a lot of fun in Marseille, between running around for business. Of course we always managed to have some fun. I took care of that. And we ate escargots in Marseille. It was so delicious, with the sauce. I will always remember that garlic sauce. Magnifique!

Nate sent a cable home, explaining a delay to his parents, that Hilda and Mendi were having difficulties. And that their problems, centered on the issuance of visas for Australia. We had the Australian Landing

Permits that we had received when we were in Munich. Our brother-in-law, Jules de Leeuw in Sydney had taken care of that part. That was the only way you could come into that country. It was the visas to get out of Europe that were the problem. And now, because Nate was there for me, I didn't have that worry. But we were trying to help my brother and sister. Our problems, Nate's and mine, were just the minor details.

The Romanian Consulate in Marseille was absolute hell. Except for one thing, that if you ever saw a gorgeous, gorgeous palace, that's what the Romanian Consulate looked like. I never saw anything like that in my whole life. I remember speaking Romanian with them, and Mendi gave me the signal to kind of slow down because he remembered the language better than I did. Because speaking five or six languages was a little bit confusing. We grew up knowing many languages. But mostly, between the three of us kids that were still left at home, we spoke Hungarian.

I think we were in Marseille for three or four days, but it seemed very much longer. Isn't it interesting how time becomes stretched out in certain circumstances? While we were there, we went to see the French HIAS in Marseille and we met a lot of French Jews that had come back from the concentration camps. They lived in Marseille in homes with the local people, because they didn't have anywhere to live. The French Jews were very congenial.[55]

After Marseille, we went back to Paris, where it was my favorite place. We were back at the California Hotel. All of the correspondence was waiting for us there, including cables from the U.S.A. and letters from consulates.[56]

It was such a heavenly feeling to go through the front door of the California Hotel, where the concierge stood, he always greeted us in French. I can remember what he looked like. He was tall, and even then his hair was a little bit grayish. Very sweet, very wonderful. We stayed in Paris through the end of July.[57]

While we were in Paris, we went to some fabulous nightclubs! We went to the Moulin Rouge.[58] Ooh Lala! The girls in the show were absolutely outrageously gorgeous. We went to the Folies Bergere, and the Lido. Also the Casino de Paris, which was very wild and intense.[59]

Oh! The women were beautiful at the Folies Bergere. They were made up with fantastic makeup. And their costumes were varied. At first they came out all dressed alike and they were dancing and kicking their legs. You could see their underpants! Then some of them changed clothes and they were dressed in very colorful costumes, with feathers and stuff. Some of them were half naked and wearing skintight outfits. Nate and Mendi went crazy! We had cocktails; I was drinking rum and Coke. I was in love with rum and Coca-Cola. And Nate was drinking anything heavy. He had a wild time in Paris. This was his third time being in Paris. He knew his way around. Before he knew me, he fooled around there a lot. He also fooled around in England. Women were available. Do you know what I mean by available? I was something new to him, because I was not available that way, not sexually. Not yet, we were not married yet!

We went dancing in Paris and that was where I saw women kissing women and dancing together. To me this was a novelty, but in Paris it was an outspoken thing and visual to your eyes.

One evening, something very unusual happened. We went to the Chinese Theatre in Paris. It was very, very different for me. I had no idea what to expect. I knew that I wanted to try Chinese food. This was a live performance theatre with a restaurant. There was a podium where the performers were up on. I couldn't stand the sounds of the music. The music was a bit too high pitched for me and I had to leave there. I would have stayed and watched the entire show but I became frustrated because I couldn't understand their language or what the play was about. I had never seen Asian people, although I knew about China from my history classes, which were mandatory in school. But I had never come face to face with Chinese people. After a while, I just had to get out of there! But oh, the food was absolutely wonderful. It was beautiful food and the first time in my life that I had ever tasted Chinese food. There was a Chinese waiter. I don't remember if he spoke French. Nate handled the situation. I don't know how he did it but there was a menu on the table. Nate started pointing to several items on the menu and somehow we got food. And the serving was first class but I didn't understand anything that was going on. I was always faced with understanding difficult languages. I was lucky that I came from an educated family but this was too much for me. After we ate, the theatre began and I couldn't take it. I started to feel claustrophobic and panicky. The moment that I stepped outside of there and I was among people, the French people that I could understand, the claustrophobic feelings disappeared. Anyway, I enjoyed the food and was happy for the experience.

And during this time Nate was constantly letting his family back home know what was going on. He sometimes sent two telegrams a day back to his parents in Mount Clemens. The whole town was on pins and needles following our story. Mount Clemens was a small town with a small Jewish community. They were tight knitted and a lot of them became emotionally involved in our story. Nate grew up there and went to school there. He had a lot of friends. They knew that Nate needed papers to take me back to the United States and that General Eisenhower had gotten involved to help us. They had made a law in America, that a GI could bring a bride back with his passport. Nate was the first one to go back to Europe to bring a war bride back! I couldn't get the visa without him. With him, I didn't need my own passport. All he needed was to show his green passport, and that was all we needed. That and the French civil marriage license and the marriage ceremony.

So you know how I feel about Paris, or how I felt before I went. It was something that a young girl would always dream about and even if you were in any other country, you would hear things about Paris. It was just something so dreamy. And when you arrive there, you already have an opinion about what the people are like, the females and the men. The men are so romantic, in just so many ways different than any men you ever meet in your whole life. I mean, you have to meet them in their own country because that is when they are more themselves. And they are very polite with the females. If someone introduces you to a Frenchman, he'll kiss your hand. They are just so lively and when you greet the morning, as you go out on the street, and you pass the stores, like pastry bakeries and cafes, you see people sitting at outside tables, drinking coffee. It is so dreamy and so romantic. And actually I met some French friends, some people that were with me at the Krupp Factory where I worked when I was in prison in Germany, and even there the French men were so very different. They just sound different. And when they are away from their own country, you can see the longing on their faces, they wish they were home. I suppose everybody feels that way. But the French are a little different. Maybe because their language is so romantic.

Some people have asked me to describe the economic environment in Paris in 1946. Did it look war-torn when I was there? Oh, but it wasn't, at all. Paris was never war-torn. Because even people that occupied the country, they were somehow aware of the City of Paris, and respected their culture, the paintings, and museums. And like I mentioned before, the bakeries and cafes were all open. And the flowers, it was summer, the flowers had just started blooming and the tulips were already completely caressing the sidewalks and the streets.

There was a movie house, it was called The Rex. We saw several movies. They didn't even have any English subtitles, everything was in French but we understood it. I remember seeing the movie, The Enchanted Cottage.

Nate's parents gave advice through cables. At one point they sent an urgent cable telling us to come home, back to Michigan, that there was work to do, that money was scarce. Yeah, and we were in Paris.

Nate didn't listen to him; he was spending money like it was growing on trees. It was his own money; from the affidavits you can see that Nate had plenty of money of his own in his bank account. So, we just kept on with what we were doing, enjoying Paris. Hey, all of us had just gotten out of a war!

The French civil marriage was very interesting.[60] The Justice of the Peace that married us performed the marriage in the courtroom. The four of us were there. It was in the morning, I think it was eleven o'clock. It was a very, very moving ceremony and I felt just absolutely elated and very happy. And then the Judge said to Nate, "And this will cost you five hundred Francs, would you please put that in the poor box?" The poor box? They probably put that in their own pockets.[61]

From the civil marriage ceremony we went out and had a gorgeous dinner. We celebrated; we had wine at the table. We were right there in the California Hotel. It was very elegant in those days; with white tablecloths and all that. It was gorgeous and we had chateaubriand and they had the most marvelous potatoes. You know how the French have the world famous sauces. Yes, delicious! You should have seen the dessert. It was a chocolate cake that I can't even explain, just the best in the world. We had the beautiful French civil ceremony and the wonderful wedding dinner. We were so very happy with how it all went, just absolutely ecstatic. Then at night, back into our bedroom, I spent my wedding night right there with the three of them: Nate, my brother, and my sister. I was so very happy! And remember, Nate had brought me a gorgeous nightgown and a matching robe, you know, for our wedding night. You are probably saying to yourself that you don't believe that we weren't alone on our wedding night. We weren't alone. It didn't happen; the marriage was not consummated, not yet! It wasn't a problem at all that I had Hilda and Mendi sleeping there because I was brought up that if you don't have a Chupa, a canopy, and if you do not break a glass, then it is not a regular Jewish wedding. According to Jewish law, I wasn't considered married, and I personally didn't consider that we were actually married yet. So nothing happened that night after the civil marriage. It didn't happen until we got to Chicago and after we celebrated our wedding completely with two hundred and fifty people that were invited.

There's one thing that I can't forget, in my travels. I looked into Nate's suitcase and he had all these gorgeous underwear and shirts, beautifully packed for his travels. I kept looking at it and telling myself that he is my husband and that we are married and I felt so proud. So thrilled, absolutely, almost unconscious with happiness!

While we were in Paris and we were already married, Abe Green sent a letter to us at the California Hotel. And Nate wouldn't let me read the letter. I'm not sure how he knew the details of my whereabouts. Nate did tell me that in the letter Abe was begging me to return the watch that Nate had given me for an engagement gift. And that he kind of ordered Nate to break it up with me. That made me sick. I was already a married woman in Paris. When Nate intercepted that letter in Paris, well, I was so glad to belong to Nate, to be protected.[62] I finally felt safe.[63]

After the wedding, Nate and I prepared ourselves to travel to Holland. We didn't leave right away, I wasn't ready, and Hilda and Mendi stayed in Paris. And now I am wondering where they lived. I was too dizzy from all the visits to the French authority offices to worry about them at that point.

Saying goodbye to Hilda and Mendi in Paris was sad. It was very sad. I was sorry leaving them but I couldn't help it because I didn't want to go to Australia, I was deadly against it. I just didn't even want to know about it. I will tell you my real feelings about leaving them, the reason I couldn't feel remorse, which I should have really, was because I wanted to erase my past. I wanted to start a new life. I could not blame myself for abandoning them. If I would have stayed with Hilda and Mendi and gone to Australia with them, I would have suffered meeting all the family. There were three other Festingers and their families living in Australia: Zsenka, Helen, and Johnny. The other sister, Aranka, was still in Romania. You know, another crying, another beginning of everything. I was tired of that. I was dying for a home; I wanted to find my own life. But I felt good about Mendi and Hilda going to Australia, because they are different than I am. And I never heard them say anything about minding going there, like I did. If I had gone to Australia, though, Hilda probably wouldn't have suffered so much there. I could have spent time helping her.

We knew that Piri, my other sister that had survived the Japanese was in Holland and I was looking forward to the reunion with her and her husband Kurt Meyers and their children. This was immense. That feeling was too big to even explain. For so long I did not know that they were alive at all, if they had survived the Japanese invasion in the East Indies. So I was out of my mind with joy. So then my thoughts went to them, hoping that I may see them before I would go to America. Nate and I flew into Holland but we almost missed the plane. We were late getting to the airport. The plane had started running without us and Nate yelled, "Stop that plane!" And he ran up to the baggage guy and took out a twenty-dollar bill and the guy somehow signaled the pilot and the plane just stopped! And then we got on. This was my first time flying on an airplane. We flew on Air France to Amsterdam.

When we arrived at the Meyers' apartment and knocked at the door, we met Kurt. That was first. I recognized Kurt because I saw him before when I was eleven years old, in Satu-Mare. That was the first and last time I had seen him, ten years before. He was so shocked when he saw us that he started yelling out, "Pirike, come on down, Nately is here!" That is what she would call him later. So she came down, and she almost fainted.

KURT: I met Nate Litvin in Amsterdam in 1946. This is how we met: one day the doorbell rang at our apartment in Amsterdam. We went to the door and standing there was Editke and Nate. It was a complete surprise! You can imagine the shock. At that point we did not know that Edith, Hilda, and Mendi Festinger were alive! We didn't know that they had survived the Nazi concentration camps.

EDITH: You can imagine the deep emotion, the joy of our reunion. Because we never thought that each of us, any of us had survived. Kurt, Piri, and their kids were living in a very decent apartment in Amsterdam. There were two little children there that I hadn't met before, Yvonne was seven and Bernie was five. They were very small when the Japanese imprisoned them. We were all hugging, kissing, and crying at the same time. It was such a big reunion because Kurt's mother and sister that had also survived the Japanese concentration camps with Piri were there. And I met Elly Olberg who was my brother Johnny's fiancée. Mr. Olberg, Ellie's father was there, too.

KURT: My sister that had survived Auschwitz had gotten this apartment ready for us, while she waited for us to arrive on the British transport ship. We got settled into life in Holland and then six months later I was finally discharged from the Dutch Army.

EDITH: We stayed at the Amstel Hotel. This time we didn't have chaperones in the hotel. But still, there had not been a Chupa, so I will tell you again: nothing happened! Nate was getting a bit anxious, but he respected my beliefs. And we went on a lot of excursions. You see Holland is like it is sunken into the water. The city of Amsterdam is surrounded by water and to go anywhere you had to take a boat, instead of a cab.[64] You can see this in the film that Nate took with his movie camera.

In Holland at that time there was not any running water to drink. Nate wrote on one of the souvenir brochure, 'Terrible, Damnable, No water to wash with.'[65] We drank bottled water, like they do here. Going on tours by boat was really interesting, tremendously so. And it was so close to the end of the war, that there was hardly any food yet. But they made the best herring right there in the house. I don't know how they made that, but I never tasted anything like that. The family cooked it, Piri and the mother-in-law. You know there are fabulous fish foods from that part of the world.

Kurt and Piri looked very sad and torn, war torn after their liberation from the Japanese. Like very fresh out of concentration camps. It was so sad. But the children did not seem sad. You know children are children. Bernie was energetic and always smiling. He looked like a happy little boy. Kurt was not working yet. But a Dutch family, a man who was very rich, befriended him. He created a business out of dealing with steel and so they made plans for Kurt to work for them.

Leaving Paris and coming into Holland was such a shock! Because it was like the whole city of Amsterdam was living in a silent war. That's what it was. The war was over and the Germans moved out of Holland but the people were so sad, completely, like they suffered a deep depression. Tremendous. Like Hilda, Mendi, and I were jolly, outgoing and we recognized that the war was over and this life was ours to use and to live. I had those feelings inside me. Every time I woke up in the morning, I thought to myself, 'It is going to be a good day, and this day is mine.' And I wasn't thinking about tomorrow, ever! My sister Pirike suffered greatly from depression from the Japanese concentration camps. She just never forgave them and she never forgot.

I also didn't forgive or forget anything. But I used it for everybody's benefit; for my family's benefit and for my neighbors. I just tell them, you have no right to go around with a sad face, if you feel sad, go home and lock the door. I get very angry with some people that keep talking about the war like it never ended. Some survivors still spend their time in the German camps talking about it. They wake up with it; they go to bed with it. I suppose different people heal and deal with stuff in different ways. You know? Some people keep their depression for their own use: to live it, to eat it, to sleep it; they internalize their depression. And some are like Hilda and I; we were happy go lucky. But the problem is, although we let the Germans go to Hell then, now we have to fight the memories, not to let the Germans into our lives now. The Dutch people were depressed because they suffered under both the Germans and the Japanese.

After our visit in Amsterdam we almost missed the flight on KLM going back to New York.[66] Perhaps they gave us one flight and there was no room on it so they canceled us. But Mr. Olberg, since he was a millionaire, he was able to get us on another flight.[67]

Kurt and Piri saw us off at the airport. Saying goodbye was very emotional. Except that I knew for sure that Nate would help me to get them to America soon. And that's exactly how it should have been and how it was, and happy ever after!

We had boarded the plane in Amsterdam, and our seats were in the back. There was a lot of noise on the plane. Because we were situated in the back of the plane it was tremendously noisy from the engines. But it was a fabulous, fabulous feeling. I felt like, that day, it was my other day of liberation. I could hear bells ringing in my ears, just like I heard the bells ringing back in Germany, just as if it was the day I was liberated. I was twenty-one years and I was on my way with my new husband to America. When I was thinking of the people that I was going to meet, I didn't even have the feeling of fear from meeting strange people, strange in-laws, and all that. I just thought to myself, I will just enjoy the present. I wasn't going to worry about what would happen when I would arrive in America, and meet all those people.

I really was out of my mind with happiness and with Nate, my husband. I really considered myself as being madly in love. I knew at that point that I had ended up with the right man! Yes, I definitely was in love and finally happy. And I was finally thinking of my future life.

There was an interesting group of musicians on the plane. I wasn't sure of who they were, but Nate said that they were a fabulous band that we had danced to at the Sea House in Munich. And there were movies on the plane. It was not a direct flight to New York and we had some stops in different countries.

The first stop was in Ireland. We got off the plane in Ireland and had a chance to taste Irish food. And the Irish food was schlachsome, fearsome, bad! And another stop was where the people wore the skirts, Scotland. Their food was treacherous. And then in the London airport, that's another terrible food. Maybe it was the fact that the war was over, sort of after starvation?

Back on the airplane, going toward New York the food was wonderful. They served from a beautiful menu during the main part of the journey, which was from London to New York.[68] It was very nice. We enjoyed it. We were very exhausted and slept a lot on the plane.

On that day when we landed in New York, there was a lot of commotion in the area where we had gotten off the plane. I said to Nate, "Who are all those people reaching out for? They have cameras on them!" And they were looking toward us. And he said, "Well, you will see for yourself." He didn't want to tell me. He was going to surprise me. And I was thinking that it had to be the musicians that were on the airplane, Nate had recognized them and I knew they were a very famous orchestra that had gone overseas to entertain the soldiers. And we were all standing in the same area. And instead of the reporters and photographers turning towards the people from the orchestra they looked at me and one of them introduced himself to me. And he said, "Why don't you follow us?" He pointed to Nate and me, and we followed him into a room. One of them asked me to sit on top of the table so everybody could see me.

I was absolutely shocked, and so elated because I remembered that for someone to be in my shoes it had to be somebody really famous to be greeted by people like that. I didn't know what kind of a celebrity I was. I didn't feel like one. And finally, the reporter started asking me questions about who am I and what was my name, and where am I from? Then I started to answer his questions and the other reporters started in and that is when the questions really began. That I was in Auschwitz concentration camp and who my family was, and I told them they were slaughtered and they took out notebooks and they started writing and scribbling. By that time I was really happy, tremendously happy. I really forgot where I came from and I didn't know where I was going. I just knew I was in a very famous room and the famous person was me. They said that I was the first war bride to come to America after the enactment of the new War Bride Law.

After we got out of the airport, Nate pulled out a little notebook that was in his pocket and he took out the name of somebody. We went to this place and he was a relative who had invited us to stay with him. He was a cousin of the family, of one of Nate's sister-in-laws. And this guy, he was just so darling, he invited us to stay with him at his house, at his apartment in New York City. It was really a wonderful apartment. It was very neat, like you'd expect a bachelor's apartment to be. He was a photographer, so you saw a lot of cameras there. And because he was a photographer we got wonderful studio photographs while we were in New York.

Being in America was such a different feeling because of the tremendous buildings, the skyscrapers. They pointed out the Empire State Building to me on that first evening when we went out into the city. Nate's cousin took us out to a kosher place, a Jewish restaurant. He knew that Nate liked to eat kosher food. And when we got there and sat down at a table, the waiter asked me what I would like to have. Usually when we went to a restaurant, Nate always ordered, like a gentleman would. And so Nate told the waiter that I had just come out of a concentration camp and it was the first day, for me, here in New York. And so when the waiter heard where I came from, he suddenly turned to everybody in the restaurant and announced, "This girl just came out of the concentration camp and married this young man, a GI!" Then everybody turned to me and started applauding and yelling out, "Mazel Tov, Mazel Tov!" They were all yelling, clapping, and talking loud and I was starving, and Nate said to the waiter, "Can I order the food now?" And so he ordered boiled chicken and sweet corn for me. That was what I wanted to eat because that was the last meal I had with my parents back home. And I was dreaming about that. And to this day those are still my favorite foods. And so there was big joy in this restaurant, and I thought to myself if I ever have children, I am going to tell my children this story.

After the meal, we went downtown to Times Square. And when I saw all the signs lit up announcing the movies that were playing, then I remembered that I saw that back home in the movie house. And I couldn't believe that I was here in person. Then we went to the Copacabana Club for drinks. It was fantastic, but we didn't stay too long, because we were so tired. We knew that we would come back to New York City and have all the time in the world to see more of this beautiful city.

I was overwhelmed when I saw the Statue of Liberty. France actually donated it as a present to the United States. They sent that lady, the Statue of Liberty over. I remembered that I wanted to see it when I would come here because of Emma Lazarus' poem on it.[69] I always loved poetry and this was one of my favorites...'Give me your tired, your poor, your huddled masses yearning to breathe free...' And then I started sobbing bitterly. And I couldn't believe it, that I didn't have to yearn any more. I was free here in the United States.

The next day we went around New York sightseeing and did a bit of celebrating. But by then I was very overwhelmed by everything. I was exhausted from the flight; I think it had taken about twenty-four hours. We had to stay in New York for a few days, and just rest up. I believe that I was exhausted not just from the flight, but the entire incredible journey of my life so far. But I was not thinking back to Europe at all; I had left Europe behind. I knew one thing; I never wanted to go back. But that didn't include France. By all means, France was number one on the list that I wanted to go back to.

And at this point Nate and I still had not had our honeymoon! No, we had not yet had our honeymoon night. My hopes were about to become worthwhile. The best was yet to come.

United Nations Relief and Rehabilitation Headquarters
Munich, 1945-1946

Edith and Hilda Festinger at Munich Post Exchange, 1946

Edith Festinger in UNRRA uniform, Munich 1945

Hilda Festinger in UNRRA uniform, Munich 1945

OFFICE OF THE CHIEF OF STAFF
WASHINGTON

17 June 1946

Dear Mr. Litvin:

General Eisenhower has asked me to tell you that he appreciates the concern which prompted your recent telegram.

As military approval of your passport application is under exclusive jurisdiction of the European Theater commander, your message has been forwarded to General McNarney in order that it may receive consideration at the earliest practicable date.

Sincerely,

JAMES STACK
Lt. Colonel, ADC
Aide to General Eisenhower

Mr. Nathan Litvin
76 Floral
Mt. Clemens, Michigan

Letter to Nate Litvin from Lt. Colonel James Stack,
Aide to General Eisenhower
June 17, 1946

WESTERN UNION

1201

CLASS OF SERVICE		SYMBOLS
This is a full-rate Telegram or Cablegram unless its deferred character is indicated by a suitable symbol above or preceding the address.		DL=Day Letter
		NL=Night Letter
		LC=Deferred Cable
		NLT=Cable Night Letter
A. N. WILLIAMS PRESIDENT		Ship Radiogram

The filing MCH7/28 MTCLEMENS MICH 43 27 it of origin. Time of receipt is STANDARD TIME at point of destination

NLT EDITH FESTINGER HIAS MILITARY 2603
CARE UNRRA DIST 5 HQ MUNICH=

I LEAVE BY PLANE FROM NEWYORK JULY 5 FOR PARIS I
HAVE ALL TRANSPORTATION BY PLANE ARRANGED WE WILL
BE MARRIED AT ONCE WAIT FOR ME IN PARIS LOVE=

NATE.

THE COMPANY WILL APPRECIATE SUGGESTIONS FROM ITS PATRONS CONCERNING ITS SERVICE

WESTERN UNION

1201

(22)

CLASS OF SERVICE		SYMBOLS
This is a full-rate Telegram or Cablegram unless its deferred character is indicated by a suitable symbol above or preceding the address.		DL=Day Letter
		NL=Night Letter
		LC=Deferred Cable
		NLT=Cable Night Letter
A. N. WILLIAMS PRESIDENT		Ship Radiogram

The filing time shown in the date line on telegrams and day letters is STANDARD TIME at point of origin. Time of receipt is STANDARD TIME at point of destination

Z49 INTL=CD MUNICH VIA WUCABLES 29 ND

VLT NATHAN LITVIN=   1946 JUL 2 AM 10 22

46 FLORAL AVE (MM QY IN ADDS 76 FITORAL AVE) MTCLEMENS
(MICH)=

I AM LEAVING TOMORROW 2ND JULY FOR PARIS IF WE GO TO
MARSEILLE YOU FIND OUR ADDRESS IS HIAS PARIS LOVE=

EDITH.

46 2 HIAS

THE COMPANY WILL APPRECIATE SUGGESTIONS FROM ITS PATRONS CONCERNING ITS SERVICE

Edith Festinger (4th from left), Hilda Festinger (2nd from right), and Mendi Festinger (kneeling on left) Munich Train Station, July 1946

Nate Litvin, La Guardia Airport, New York, July 5, 1946

Friday, July 26, 1946

IT HAPPENED IN PARIS . . .

Veteran Nate Litvin of Mt. Clemens has returned to Paris by plane, this time..to marry Edith Festinger, a Romanian girl who had been a Nazi slave for two years.

Litvin met the young woman while with the Army of Occupation in Munich. She had survived two years of Nazi brutality and her parents had been fed into the incinerators of a murder camp.

Now as a civilian, Litvin plans to marry her and bring her back with him as his wife—free from any immigration quota restrictions.

Litvin was active in AZA and Bnai Brith work in Mt. Clemens before entering the service.

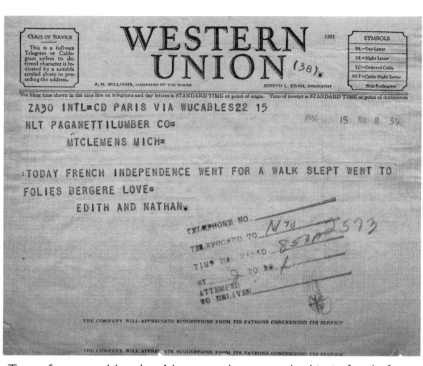

Two of many cables that Nate sent home to the Litvin family from
Europe July 1946

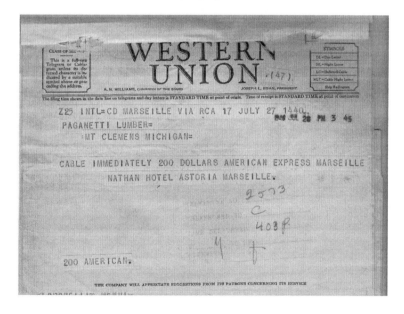

Part 4

Epilogue

Edith and Nate were married in an Orthodox Jewish wedding ceremony on August 25, 1946, in Chicago, Illinois under the Chupa. The film footage and wedding album of that day shows the two hundred and fifty guests, consisting of family and friends. After a solemn religious ceremony, there is incredible dancing and kissing, celebrating the great love and joy for these newlyweds, Nathan and Edith Litvin, soul mates who found each other after the Holocaust and had hope for the future. The sheer joy depicted in the films represents a triumph over adversity.

૭૭

MENDI: After Edith and Nathan went to America, Hilda and I flew to Holland, met up with Piri, her husband Kurt Meyers, and their two small children. Hilda and I were staying with my brother Johnny's fiancée Elly Olberg, and her father, in their beautiful home in Amsterdam. We tried to get exit visas there, but that didn't work out either. We spent four weeks in Holland and then returned to Paris.

We had to wait in Paris for six months until finally we got our visas. The Jewish organizations were very good to us, and to hundreds of others. While Hilda and I were in Paris for six months, they got us into a hotel, the Hotel Continental. They arranged for us a place where we could go to eat every day, we went there once or twice but we didn't like the food so we found other arrangements. For those who couldn't pay at all, the Joint Distribution Committee paid for everything. For those of us who had relatives, we borrowed, and my brother-in-law Jules paid back everything. There were two fellows who were brothers that were traveling to Australia. They had American dollars and they gave us an address in Sydney, where my brother-in-law could send the money and when the fellows arrived in Australia they were paid back.

I met up with Hoffman the Kapo in Paris. The day before Hilda and I finally left Paris, we met a friend from Satu-Mare and he was sitting in a café with that Hoffman and a woman. My friend introduced me to Hoffman; he called him Dr. Hoffman. He wasn't a doctor at all. We told our friend who that man was and Hilda and I went to the police, and we told them the name of the hotel where Hoffman lived. They told us that we had to go the police station nearer to that hotel. We didn't have time to do that because it was already perhaps eleven or twelve o'clock at night and we had to leave the next morning. I don't know what happened to Hoffman after that.

Jules had tried to book us on a plane to Australia, but that didn't work. And we missed the first ship going to Australia, the Johann DeWitt because we couldn't get the visa in time to come on that ship. But we got on the second one, which was a cargo ship, the SS Monkay. The conditions on the Monkay were very bad and I nearly set the ship on fire.

The trip lasted three months. It took us to Saigon,[70] and we had to wait six weeks there whilst the ship took arms to the French fighting up north. We didn't know that at the time. Hilda and I arrived in Australia on the 11th of February 1947.

January 23, 1947
To: Hilda Festinger
C/O Messageries Maritimes
S.S. Monkay, Saigon Indochina
My dear Hilda & Mendi,

We received your letter and are indeed sad that you are having so much trouble. I can't understand why they don't arrange plane tickets for you. We understand that Ishmayo is going to Australia to marry you.[71] By your letter you don't seem to be in love with him. If not, you should write him to wait awhile before he makes the trip with his mother to Australia.

Now if after you are in Australia and you don't like it, you can come to America as a tourist and maybe find a boy for yourself & stay here. I know that Editke will be very happy if you are near her in America.

Enclosed is five dollars. Maybe it will help you a little.

Love, Nathan

(Letter was returned to Nate in Mount Clemens, unopened with nine postmarks)

MENDI: After I arrived in Australia, my brother Johnny and I went into business together in Freeman's Reach. It was an orchard with fifteen hundred orange trees and plenty of land to build for rabbits but we also built sheds for chickens, which I loved too. The first batch of chickens was about eight hundred and I would get up very early in the morning and check on them. We did very well with the chickens, we got up to two thousand five hundred of them for laying eggs. And as for the Angora rabbits; we had built a special shed for the rabbits, a huge shed. I started with a half a dozen rabbits and started to breed them and bred up to about a hundred. We couldn't get the wool spun in Australia. That was the problem.

KURT: I had found a job in Amsterdam through a friend at a metal smelting factory. I worked my way up and after six months I became the manager. And then the company was sold. It was the Hollandia Steel Company that took over the smelting company. Then I had a new boss. He liked me and invited me to dinner. He then told me, "We want to open a business in America, are you interested to go anywhere in America?" I said, "Yes, I would go anywhere in America."

Edith and Nate had left to go to Michigan and they got married. They sent us many packages from America with food. My brother-in-law Nate sent us the affidavits that we needed to get our visas to come to the United States.

We received our visas to come to the United States at the end of 1947. So in 1948 we went to Michigan. We waited three months with Editke and Nate in Mount Clemens, until my company found a place to open in Binghamton, New York. That was where we ended up.

EDITH: I tried to imagine if Nate had not come back for me, how I would have handled the situations and you know what? You'd better believe me when I tell you this, to actually close this whole subject. I would have survived! Just like I survived the whole goddamned concentration camp. I don't know how I would have done it, but I wouldn't have been in misery. I was free and not in prison anymore.

And besides, that part is over. So I don't have to worry about it anymore.

Mr. and Mrs. Baruch Litvin
request the honor of your presence
at the marriage of their son

Nathan

to

Edith Festinger
from Transylvania, Roumania
on Sunday, the Twenty-fifth of August
nineteen hundred and forty-six
Ceremony five-thirty in the afternoon
Dinner following
at Congregation Ateres Zion
1148-50 N. Spaulding
Chicago, Illinois

Nate and Edith Litvin, under the Chupa Chicago,
Illinois, August 25, 1946

Kurt, Piri, Bernard, and Yvonne Meyers
Mount Clemens, Michigan, 1948

Hilda Festinger, Sydney, Australia, 1947

Mendi Festinger, with his Angora pet rabbit,
Snow Ball, Sydney, Australia, 1950's

Edith Festinger Litvin lives in Northern California, where she knits and sells colorful, ecologically friendly shopping bags.

Hilda Festinger Graham lives in Sydney, Australia

Nate Litvin died unexpectedly in 1993, in Walnut Creek, California, at the age of seventy-two

Kurt Meyers died in 2005, in Binghamton, New York, at the age of ninety-five. Piri Festinger Meyers survives him.

Mendi Festinger died in 2007, in East Killara, Australia, at the age of eighty-seven.

Part 5

Glossary

Borscht: Beet and flanken meat soup, flavored with onion and spices.

Challah: Braided egg bread for the Sabbath, in Yiddish.

Chupa: Canopy under which the bride and groom must stand, which symbolizes the home that will be shared, in Yiddish.

Goulash: Hungarian stew with beef, potatoes, tomato sauce, salt, paprika, and garlic.

Grevins: Cooked chicken skin that becomes crunchy when fried with onions, in Yiddish.

India: Indonesia was referred to as India.

Jumper: Australian slang for a knitted sweater.

ke: Hungarian endearment added as a suffix to a name: i.e. Editke means Edith darling.

Kishke: Sausage stuffed food, in Yiddish.

L'Chaim: Toast: 'To life,' in Hebrew.

Mamaliga/Pulishka: Romanian/Hungarian translation for corn meal or polenta.

Mazel Tov: Congratulations, in Yiddish.

Paprikash: A Hungarian stew with chicken, rice, tomato sauce, garlic, salt, and paprika.

Pena: Vagina or female parts, in Hungarian.

Pish: To urinate, in Hungarian.

Rebbe: Rabbi, in Yiddish.

Rumania, Roumania, Romania: Spelling of the country where Transylvania is located, during different historical eras.

Satmar/Szatmar: Hungarian spelling/pronunciation of Romanian City Satu-Mare.

Shabbos: Jewish Sabbath, in Yiddish; in Hebrew it is pronounced Shabbot.

Shadduch: An arranged marriage, in Yiddish.

Shana madel: Pretty girl, in German or Yiddish.

Shlachsome: Bad or rotten tasting food, in Yiddish.

Shmaltz: A butter substitute made out of chicken fat, in Yiddish. It is used because the kosher dietary laws prohibit mixing meat and butter/dairy.

Shtuberdeenz: Room servant, in German.

Shule: Synagogue, in Yiddish.

Swarze links: Black hair, in German.

Touchas or tushy: Ass or buttocks, in Yiddish.

Yiddish: The Jewish language, derived from German and written in Hebrew letters.

Yudah: Jew, in German.

Afterword

NAOMI: Sometimes when she naps in the afternoon, I hear her cry out. It's a scream that originates from that place in her brain where the memories live. I run to her and gently shake her awake. "Mom, it's just a dream," I say, as I check to see that her breath and heartbeat have normalized. She is eighty-five now.

I have those dreams, too. They are her memories, which permeated the soft boundaries of my childhood self and now live in that place in my brain too.

I don't remember how old I was when the haunting began, with their sounds and sights and smells. I became aware that life wasn't safe. The fear never goes away. I have tried to become adept at lucid dreaming, so that when the Nazis come for me at night, I can fly away.

I always intended to tell the family story. I knew that the beauty of the love story between my parents would shine through, while remembering the horrific legacy of mass murder and hatred that still threatens us today.

Acknowledgments

NAOMI: I began this project attempting to find a way to honor my mother, Edith, and my father, Nathan. My father had died suddenly in 1993, and twelve years had gone by. I had all of my mother's original poetry, her essays, and her photo albums, along with my own store of notes from stories told and old college papers. I had written just one page of my book over thirty years ago, from one of my mother's experiences that she had plucked out, shocking me on a day that I can't remember.

One day shortly before my Dad's untimely death, I had felt the urgency to interview him as we sat in the cab of a pickup truck, taking a break outside our family bagel factory. Hastily scribbling the precious information on paper, I added the interview to my stockpile of stuff that I would someday use to transform my family's true legends into written history.

My father's cache was unearthed one day as I was cleaning out closets. His scrapbook jammed with archival documents, mementos, photos, and the old 8 mm. movie projector transfixed me as I realized that there was no turning back. I slipped into the vortex of this book, surrendering myself to the process.

The most credible, live resource, my mother Edith Festinger Litvin, has been a great partner, emotionally available, and by my side during the entire time as this work blossomed and also became a stunning personal odyssey for me.

My darling uncles: Kurt Meyers, from Binghamton, New York, and Mendi Festinger, from East Killara, Australia, both died during the writing of this book, before they could see the flowers of our efforts. My uncles contributed their masculine voices by telephone, video, mail, and email interviews. My beautiful, blonde Aunty Hilda supplied her voice by responding in an eloquently handwritten letter from her home in Sydney, Australia. Kurt's wife, my Tonti Piri was right next to him during the telephone conversations as he told me his stories and then mailed his autobiography to me.

As I researched related issues and searched for answers to nagging mysteries, I found people that generously and graciously gave me information: Dr. Ken Lury; my Aussie cousins: Greta Festinger, Robbie Festinger, Monica Graham, Marilyn and Geoff Rosenbaum. My Dad's brother, Emanuel Litvin (Uncle Manny) and cousin Danny Litvin contributed essential Litvin family history. My friend Ruthanne Martin translated French documents, Lisa Hollo supported me with her ongoing friendship, Dave Glass did photographic repair, and Janice Litvin for final editing.

Three people came into my life that were instrumental to the creation of this book: Peter Handel, Doris Ober, and Sir Martin Gilbert. I am eternally grateful to Peter for letting me into his office with my 'kitchen sink'. Peter told me what to do with it, and has continued to share his ongoing expertise. When I approached Doris Ober for manuscript consultation, what she gave me back was a gift. Sir Martin Gilbert, who, after reading my manuscript urged me to publish, and continued to give me hope and validation throughout my long publishing quest, has rewarded me by writing the foreword for this book.

Notes

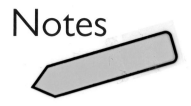

CHAPTER ONE

[1] Hershmila Festinger, thirteen, and a cousin were in a small boat on the Tisza River when the boat began to take on water. As the boat was sinking, Hershmila started yelling out to Romanians on the riverbank, "I cannot swim, save my life because my father is rich! He is going to give you lots of money." The Romanians hollered back, "Let the Jew drink." The boys drowned.

[2] 2008: The Hotel Tisza, Sighet: "There aren't many choices - at least not in Sighet. One option is the Hotel Tisza right in the middle of town. It's an old, time-honored hotel. A double room with balcony and bathroom costs 450,000 Lei per person, including breakfast. Since staff at the hotel tends to forget to tell it to the customers, I should better mention it here: There's no running water at all between midnight and 5 am..." (Excerpt from the Internet)

[3] Hosszumeszu, Hungary, in Romanianian is known as Campulong LaTisa.

[4] The Singing Fool (Warner Brothers, 1928), a box office record breaker, is a very good follow-up to the historic first talkie of The Jazz Singer (Warner Brothers 1927), starring Broadway star Al Jolson.

CHAPTER TWO

[5] The Royal Netherlands East Indies Army.

[6] Rabbi Teitelbaum, an anti-Zionist, was able to get out because a deal had been struck between a Hungarian Zionist official, Rudolph Kastner, a Nazi collaborator and a deputy of Adolf Eichmann. Kastner intended to rescue only Hungarian Zionists that could pay, on a special train bound for Switzerland but then other religious

Jews were also included. The train course was changed by the Germans and sent to Bergen-Belsen, where they reportedly received special treatment as almost 1,700 passengers waited for further negotiations between rescue activists and the Nazi leadership. In the end, the train was released and continued on to Switzerland. Kastner was assassinated in Israel in 1947. Teitelbaum went to Israel in 1946 but then settled in Brooklyn, New York and died there in 1979.

[7] 2008: Just off the Piata, at Str. Bessarabia 10, is the Synagogue. Sighet was the birthplace of 1986 Nobel Prize winner, writer Elie Wiesel and the house on Str. Tudor Vladimirescu where he spent his childhood is a memorial museum. On Str. Muresan, off Piata Libertatii is a large monument commemorating the Jews who were deported in 1944 by the ruling Hungarians. (Excerpt from the Internet)

[8] In 1941, forced Jewish labor, after two years of implementation, acquired a more punitive character.

CHAPTER THREE

[9] Ghetto Conference.

[10] According to information gathered from the Final Report of the International Commission on the Holocaust in Romania, presented to Romanian President Ion Iliescu, November 11, 2004, Bucharest, Romania.

[11] Information gathered from United States Holocaust Memorial Museum's website.

[12] In 2006 Makarov, Ukraine had a population of approximately 9,000.

[13] At Ellis Island, the spelling of Lettvin became Litvin for some of the family. The Litvin/Lettvin family history is courtesy of Emanuel Litvin.

[14] The Carpathia, built for the British Cunard Line in 1903 for Liverpool-New York and Trieste-New York service, later rescued seven hundred and five survivors on April 15, 1912 from the sunken Titanic. Then, in 1918 the Carpathia was torpedoed and sunk by a German submarine off the English coast.

[15] From 1867 through 1918 Trieste flourished as part of the Austro-Hungarian Empire and was Central Europe's prosperous Mediterranean seaport and its capital of literature and music. Between 1895-1918 Trieste was at the border between Italy and Slovenia. Trieste became part of Italy in 1920.

[16] Letter to Naomi Litvin from Baruch Litvin in 1969: To our dear Grand Child Naomi: Dearest Naomi, Shalom: We thought during the Thanksgiving season to pen down part of your Zeide and Baba's experience for which we ought to be thankful. We also thought it would be worthwhile for you to read it and keep it...Kislev 8, 1969 On This Day We Were Married 60 Years Ago: Today's Letter's Heading Is: Who Would Have Believed? As Stated in Isaiah Chapter 53, Verse One: Who would have believed 63 years ago upon landing in New York without a hat (it was blown off by walking from one railroad car to another on the way to the boat through Austria Hungary) and HIAS the organization that was taking care of immigrants of my type that had nobody in America, took me over to an address that I have been given, and upon coming in to his house said, "You can stay with me for one week, then you must go." Where would I go? That today I am, what I am? Who would have believed that after six months being in New York, and months of investigation for my application at the Industrial Removal Office (an organization for removing immigrants from new York), I was sent to Chicago and shipped on a freight train without given something to eat during the three days traveling from New York to Chicago and accidentally arrived in Chicago on the same day as Mother has arrived...Who would have believed that in the great crash of the Banks in 1929 we went on a farm and lost seventy-one thousand dollars in cash, incurring debts, becoming almost beggars, or better, became "Creators that were once Man" and did get back on our feet?...

[17] The Purple Gang was a ruthless mob of Jewish bootleggers and hijackers that had the run of Detroit in the 1920s and early 1930s. Detroit was a major port for smuggling alcohol during Prohibition, being on the border with Canada.

[18] Inside the Clemension, the 1939 Mount Clemens High School yearbook, Nate says in the Will, 'I, Nate Litvin, bequeath my excellent debating ability to anyone who simply **must** have the last word.'

[19] From a 1938 Mount Clemens Daily Leader newspaper article, '…Nate Litvin walked home twelve miles from school after strenuous football practice…Nate, who is the only Jewish member of the Mount Clemens' squad…after football practice he trudges homeward to the farm of his parents…'

[20] The 1942 archival film footage of Paganetti Lumber Basketball Team in their locker room features one of the members dancing nude.

[21] Theresienstadt was a transit camp for Czech Jews. It was a ghetto labor camp based on age, disability due to military service, or celebrity. The Nazis used Theresienstadt to hide the premeditated mass murder of Jewish populations.

[22] Zyklon B, previously used for fumigation, was being used at Auschwitz, as the Nazis searched for the fastest gassing method. Up to 6,000 Jews per day were gassed.

[23] In 2004, the Claims Conference paid 2,488 Jewish victims of Nazi medical experiments '… In researching the claims for this program, the Claims Conference uncovered much new evidence about medical experiments under the Third Reich that had not been previously documented. For example, injection of Bromide, a chemical substance, was mentioned among many women who were incarcerated in Auschwitz as the cause for their loss of menstruation and in some cases also their fertility. While there was no written documentation regarding such experiments, the number of applicants mentioning this chemical substance led to the recognition by the

German Foundation of this Nazi program as a medical experiment...' Edith Festinger Litvin missed the deadline to file for this medical experiment award; not realizing that the 'Brohm' added to the soup was considered a medical experiment.

[24] The Dupont Mission was an operation by the United States and British OSS (Secret Operations Group) led by Navy Lieutenant Jack H. Taylor, USNR. In his report dated 30 May 1945, he wrote the full and complete debriefing about his parachuting into Nazi controlled Austria, near the Hungarian border on 13 October 1944, and his subsequent capture by Nazis and incarceration in Mauthausen. Lt. Taylor was liberated from Mauthausen on 5 May 1945 by American forces. His description of Mauthausen and events are extremely similar to Mendi Festinger's account of Mauthausen and the sub-camps. They could have crossed paths.

[25] The commandant of Melk was Obersturmbannfuhrer Julius Ludolf. At some period the infamous Untersturmannfuhrer Streitwieser held command. The construction works were under the supervision of Obergruppenfuhrer Kammler and Obersturmfuhrer Schulz. Ludolf was hanged in April 1947, but Streitwieser, Kammler, and Schultz escaped.

CHAPTER FOUR

[26] HASAG (Hugo Schneider Aktiengesellschaft-Metalwarenfabrik, Leipzig) is a privately held German company that is still in business to this day. Their website includes an admission of guilt for the use of slave labor during World War II.

[27] A letter from Germany, received by Edith Litvin in 1974, asked for her participation in a war crimes investigations case: '...Dear Mrs. Litvin-Festinger, Prisoner killings perpetrated in compounds centered around the main concentration camp of Buchenwald are the criminal acts I am at the moment inquiring into...One of those compounds was set up in Altenburg/Thuringen and you were, according to my information, one of those persons kept there under National Socialist terror orders...Should you be willing to answer the questions...'

[28] On May 10, 2001 a United States federal judge dismissed lawsuits that had blocked payments from a $5 billion German fund set up in 2000 to pay reparations to one million people that were slave laborers during the Nazi regime. Edith received a one-time payment of $7,500 for being a slave laborer at the Krupp Factory.

[29] Nathan Litvin received a letter dated August 15, 1946 from Jack Clark, along with a photo of The Krupp Factory in Altenburg, Germany. Edith had already left on the death march when Jack Clark's regiment captured Altenburg. '…My regiment captured Altenburg and I am enclosing a picture taken in one of the building[s] at the factory. Just thought you might be interested in seeing it. The object in the center is a concrete pillbox…'

[30] They walked from Altenburg, Thuringia to Meerane, Silesia for five days and five nights with no food or water. The actual distance was about seventy miles. The march from Altenburg to Meerane ended on April 13, 1945.

[31] Although there are some instances of Israelis seeking revenge on Nazi war criminals, for the most part, the Holocaust Survivors just wanted to get on with their lives.

[32] 77 pounds.

CHAPTER FIVE

[33] In 1941 President Franklin D. Roosevelt had asked that private organizations handle the on-leave recreation needs of the U.S. armed forces. Six civilian agencies coordinated their efforts and formed the USO (United Service Organizations). The Salvation Army, Young Men's Christian Association, Young Women's Christian Association, National Catholic Community Services, National Travelers Aid Association, and the National Jewish Welfare Board formed the USO as a private, nonprofit organization.

[34] AFN Munich, The Armed Forces Network, signed on the air on June 8, 1945 as Radio Munich. Soon after AFN Frankfurt, AFN Bremen, and AFN Berlin joined the network.

[35] Munich was the birthplace of the Nazi Party, the ideological center of the Third Reich. Meetings of the Nazi Party at the Lowenbrau Keller and other beer gardens had incited the masses of Munich's poorer classes.

CHAPTER SIX

[36] This is the same Herschowitz that Mendi Festinger encountered as a Kapo in Ebensee.

[37] Character's name has been changed.

[38] Feldafing in Munich was the first all-Jewish Displaced Persons camp. Feldafing opened right after liberation, in May of 1945.

[39] V-J Day, Victory over Japan was August 15, 1945.

[40] The purpose of UNRRA was for repatriation and support of refugees and countries that had been under Nazi control and would come under Allied control at the end of the war. In October 1945 UNRRA assumed responsibility for Displaced Persons. By the summer of 1946 it cared for 850,000 people. They had a staff of 25,000 people and were helped by voluntary agencies, such as the American Jewish Joint Distribution Committee (JDC), the Jewish Agency and its military arm, the Haganah, The Hebrew Immigrant Aid Society (HIAS), The Jewish Committee for Relief Abroad, Organization for Rehabilitation and Training (ORT), and Vaad Hatzalah (The Orthodox Jewish Rescue Committee). In the summer of 1947, UNRRA's functions ended. The care of displaced persons was then transferred to the new International Refugee Organization.

[41] Effective 23 May 1946, Edith's UNRRA Transfer Slip for reassignment to HIAS stated that her position was Grade 3 Interviewer.

[42] 25 June 1946: TO WHOM IT MAY CONCERN: Miss Edith Festinger and Miss Hilda Festinger have been purchasing rations and gift items from the supplies in the Munich Post Exchange and have permission to carry these items with them. MUNICH POST EXCHANGE, Sales Store-Mgr. Norma Wilmer.

[43] There is a documented criticism of UNRRA's power grabbing contained in the Gershon Gelbert report on conditions at Feldafing Displaced Persons Camp which was found in Nate Litvin's scrapbook. An article by Howard Byrne (Life Begins Anew for Feldafing DPs) from the Stars and Stripes military newspaper was found with the Feldafing report, and this material was donated to the United States Holocaust Museum in Washington, DC.

[44] On May 9, 2005, Edith Litvin received the following information from the Claims Conference on Material Claims Against Germany: ... "GOLD TRAIN" SETTLEMENT WILL FUND SERVICES FOR HUNGARIAN HOLOCAUST SURVIVORS.... 'A Settlement has been preliminarily approved by U.S. District Judge Patricia Seitz in a class-action lawsuit brought by Jewish Hungarian victims of Nazism and heirs of Hungarian Nazi victims against the United States government regarding the handling of property contained on the "Hungarian Gold Train," in the U.S. District Court for the Southern District of Florida. The case, known as Rosner v. United States, was originally filed in May 2001...The Hungarian Gold Train consisted of approximately 24 freight cars that contained personal property stolen or otherwise taken from Hungarian Jews during World War II by the Nazi regime and its collaborationist Hungarian government. The train came into the custody of the U.S. military in Austria at the conclusion of the war. The lawsuit alleges that the United States mishandled the contents of the train, but the United States denies any legal liability in the handling of the Hungarian Gold Train property. As part of the Settlement, the U.S. government has agreed to pay up to $25.5 million of which approximately $21 million will be used to fund social service projects benefiting eligible class members... The U.S. government will pay another $500,000 to create an archive of documents and materials relating to the Hungarian Gold Train and the looting of the Hungarian Jewish community... Class Members included in the Settlement are Jews that were born before May 8, 1945 who lived in the 1944 borders of Greater Hungary some time between 1939 and 1945 and the heirs of Hungarian Jewish Nazi victims...'

[45] From Email correspondence from Captain John Lury's son, Dr. Ken Lury to Naomi Litvin (2005) '…I have a book detailing the men and travels of my father's battalion during the war and a Croix de Guerre certificate he received from the King of Belgium…I frequently look at the picture of your mother and my father and marvel at how happy they look together. I think the answer to why he did not marry her lies in what you wrote about all the red tape and difficulty involved in your parents getting married and returning to the U.S. My father was not someone who would fight for what he wanted. He probably would have been overwhelmed at the hurdles involved and took the path of least resistance. My guess is he had many regrets about this decision…'

[46] PFC Nathan Litvin: Rifle Marksman & Supply Clerk 835. Decorations and Citations: EAME Theater Ribbon with 2 Bronze Stars, Bronze Arrowhead, and Victory Medal World War II. Battle and Campaign: Normandy, Northern France.

[47] Some of the notarized affidavits follow:
PAGANETTI LUMBER COMPANY (On company letterhead)
"The Better the Lumber The Better The Building"
Lumber – Builders' Supplies
Doors, Sash and Interior Finish
MOUNT CLEMENS, MICHIGAN
April 25, 1946
To Whom It May Concern:
This is to certify that Nathan Litvin recently returned from the U.S. Armed Forces, is a full fledged partner of the Paganetti Lumber Company, and that his ownership is to extent of one quarter (1/4) as registered according to the laws of partnership at Mount Clemens Michigan, under the laws of the State of Michigan.
Attached is a certified statement of the net worth of the company.
PAGANETTI LUMBER COMPANY.
By: B. Litvin (signed)
April 30, 1946
To the U.S. Consul,

Munich, Germany

This is to certify that Nathan Litvin formerly with The United States Army is a partner in the Paganetti Lumber Company, and since his return earning a salary of $100.00 per week in addition to dividends that may be accrued to him as a partner.

PAGANETTI LUMBER COMPANY.

By: B. Litvin (signed)

AFFIDAVIT OF SUPPORT

State of Michigan

County of Wayne

...Deponent Nathan Litvin is a citizen of the United Sates by virtue of his birth in Detroit, Michigan on January 14, 1921;

Deponent is a one-quarter partner in the Paganetti Lumber Company of Mt. Clemens, Michigan from which he derives an annual income of $5200.00; that he has on deposit to his credit at the First National Bank of Mt. Clemens $5000.00 and at the Mt. Clemens Savings Bank $1650.00; that he is the owner of the following additional resources:

U.S. War Bonds, Type E $ 5900.00

Interest in business $15000.00

... he is an honorably discharged veteran of the army of the United States and that while on active service he became acquainted with Edith Festinger who presently resides in Munich, Germany. Deponent is presently engaged to marry said Edith Festinger and is anxious to assist in her migration to the United States at the earliest possible time.... he assumes full financial responsibility for the said Edith Festinger during her residence in the United States and guarantee that she will not become a public charge; ...ready, willing and able to furnish bond in any reasonable amount if requested to do so, said bond guaranteeing that the aforesaid alien, if admitted...ready, willing and able to provide a suitable and comfortable place for said immigrant to live... This affidavit is executed for the purpose of inducing the American Consul at Munich, Germany, to issue an immigration visa to the said Edith Festinger. Nathan Litvin (signed)

Notarized 6th of June 1946

[48] Aranka Festinger, her husband Eugene Schwartz, and their son Alfred (Freddie) came to America from Romania with Nate and Edith's help in 1950.

[49] Garmisch-Partenkirchen in the Bavarian Alps is a beautiful German ski resort area. It was the site of the 1936 Winter Olympics and Hitler had allowed one token Jew, Rudi Ball, a hockey player, to participate, in order to appease the Olympic officials.

[50] Referring to Zsenka Festinger and Johnny Festinger, who survived the Japanese camps.

[51] Edith wrote her Jewish name in Hebrew letters.

[52] The U.S. Army's Counter Intelligence Corps (CIC) was assigned to track down Nazis for prosecution. The administration of justice for the Nazi murderers gave way to the recruitment of Nazis for the cold war against the Soviet Union, and also for American agencies. The most incredible case is that of Wernher von Braun, who became head of the American space program along with his space partner Arthur Randolph. Other Nazis received secret missions here and abroad.

CHAPTER SEVEN

[53] In 1939, the Orient Express trains were stopped for the war. In January 1946 service resumed with The Simplon Orient running three times per week.

[54] Twenty-five years later, in 1970, Edith and Nate returned to Paris and the same concierge was still working at the California Hotel, and they recognized each other.

[55] During the war over 77,000 Jews that were deported from France were murdered in the Nazi camps.

[56] EMBASSY OF THE UNITED STATES OF AMERICA, PARIS

26 July 1946
Madame Litvin, Edith
Hotel California, 16 Rue Berri Paris
Madam,

As a result of the steps you have taken toward the Embassy of the United States, I am eager to inform you that your request for a visa to enter the United States will be taken into consideration when you present to the Embassy a valid passport covered by a French exit visa.

It will be necessary to present to the Embassy proof that a passage has been retained for you aboard any means of transport to the United States.

Wishing you to believe, Madame, in the expression of my eminent consideration.

Robert Scheider (signed) Vice Counsel of the United States of America

[57] The hotel bills from The California Hotel, Paris, were from July 9 through July 31, 1946.

[58] The Moulin Rouge was one of many entertainment centers that had continued to function during the war in order to entertain the Nazis who gathered in Paris for rest and relaxation.

[59] One of nude dancers from Casino de Paris, Michelle Bernardini, was the model for the first bikini, which was invented in Paris in 1946.

[60] District 8 of Paris, the area around the Champs Elysees was where Nate and Edith's French Marriage License was issued on July 22, 1946.

[61] In 1946, a new French constitution established the Fourth Republic and the franc went to its lowest value.

[62] In 2005, fifty-nine years later, a second letter from Abe came for Edith Litvin '...The reason I'm writing - I met Editke Festinger while she was temporarily living in an apartment in Munich, Germany,

occupied by a German woman whose husband, a captain in the German army, was being held as a prisoner of war in England. This was back in May 1945 while I was serving in the 8th Air Force at the time. While I was in Munich, I was charged for being AWOL from my base several days. My commanding officer wanted to know where I was and why I was missing. I told him I visited a girl, a holocaust victim but it was just platonic. He said to prove my statement. So he got one of my buddies to drive us in an Army Jeep to visit Edith. Edith was able to speak in English with my Captain. Afterwards when we left, the Captain said to me that he was delightfully surprised. And I was cleared of the AWOL charge. If I am indeed correct in connecting you with Edith Festinger and Nate Litvin, then please respond as soon as possible. Thank you. Abe Green...'

[63] After settling in Mount Clemens, Michigan, Nate intercepted a letter to Edith from Katzender, who was writing to her from Israel in 1946.

[64] Archival film footage shows boat taxi rides in Amsterdam, 1946.

[65] Nate's written comments regarding the conditions in Amsterdam differed from what follows, as printed in the 1946 brochure: 'Holland stages a comeback: The Netherlands are rapidly getting back to normal, and indications are that sooner than originally expected, tourists will be able to enjoy the hospitality of the famous little land of old-world charm and modern progress. The scars of war that marred beaches, the dunes and the inundated areas are rapidly being erased. The lovely woods and lakes of Holland will soon beckon the visitor with the same irresistible allure which made her justly famous as a tourist center of world renown.'

[66] KLM Royal Dutch Airlines, The Flying Dutchman departed August 6, 1946 at 13.30 hrs. The manifest shows that Mr. and Mrs. Litvin sat in 11c and 11d. The names of the other passengers are typed on the manifest with 'Mr. and Mrs. Litvin' handwritten in pencil, above the area 'reserved for crew,' indicating a last minute adjustment.

[67] Sixty-three years later Edith found out what had happened to Johnny Festinger's wife's family during the war. Willy Olberg, the jeweler, had moved his two children, Ellie and Frans, from Amsterdam, along with supplies of diamonds and gold to Indonesia where he hoped they would be safer. Willy Olberg and his partner were running their business in Bandung. Mrs. Olberg and her aged mother had stayed behind in Amsterdam and gone into hiding. But they were betrayed and then perished. Ellie was attending school in Indonesia and her brother Frans had gone into the Dutch Air Force, serving in the East Indies. The Japanese imprisoned Willy, Ellie, and Frans.

[68] The 1946 menu onboard the KLM airliner was: 'Aperitif, Hors D'oeuvre, Petite Marmite, Caneton a L'Orange, Fromage, Fruits, Cafe et Liqueur.'

[69] Emma Lazarus, 1849-1887, was one of the first successful Jewish American authors. Her famous poem, The New Colossus, was written in 1883 and is engraved on a plaque in the Statue of Liberty. She was a powerful voice against anti-Semitism.

EPILOGUE

[70] In Saigon, Mendi and Hilda were caught up in the French Indochina War and the fall of Saigon. Fighting had broken out in November of 1946 between the Vietnamese and French troops in Haiphong.

[71] Ishmayo was a Sephardic Jew that Hilda had met on the voyage. Nate's father had hired a detective to do a background search on him. They found out that Ishmayo was 'no damn good.' The report was forwarded to Australia, and Hilda broke it off with him.

2825077

Made in the USA